The Story of The Borough
by Mary Boast

London Borough of Southwark
Neighbourhood History No. 7

ISBN 0 905849 22 1
First published in 1980
Revised edition 1997

© 1997 London Borough of Southwark

British Library Cataloguing in Publication Data

A catalogue record for this book is available from the British Library
No part of this publication may be reproduced, stored in a retrieval system or transmitted by any means without prior permission of the Library and Information Services Manager

Cover illustrations
Front cover: Borough High Street, watercolour by William Knox, 1826*.
Inside front cover: An aerial view of Roman Southwark by Peter Froste.
Inside back cover: Southwark Town Hall, Borough High Street, 1828.
*By courtesy of the Fine Art Society, London.

Contents

	Introduction	
1	Roman Southwark	1
2	The Borough	3
3	The Borough Inns	5
4	Southwark Fair and Borough Market	8
5	Crime and Punishment	10
6	Old Prisons	12
7	Two Great Hospitals	14
8	St George the Martyr Church and Parish	17
9	John Harvard	20
10	Documentaries	21
11	A Place to Live	23
12	Schools, Old and New	25
13	Shops and Trades	27
14	Two World Wars	30
15	A Borough Panorama	32
	Booklist	
	Index	

Key to the map

1 Former St Thomas' church and
   Old Operating Theatre
2 War Memorial, site of St Margaret's Church
3 King's Head Yard
4 White Hart Yard
5 George Inn
6 Site of Tabard Inn
7 Calvert's Buildings
8 Hop Exchange
9 King's Arms PH
10 St Saviour's and St Joseph's Schools
11 Octavia Hill Cottages
12 Brandon House, site of Suffolk Place
13 John Harvard and Local Studies Library,
   site of Marshalsea Prison
14 St Hugh's Church, Charterhouse-in-Southwark
15 Mint Street Adventure Playground, site of workhouse
16 Charles Dickens School
17 Scovell Estate, site of King's Bench Prison
18 Police Station, site of 'Stone's End'
19 Henry Wood Hall, former Holy Trinity Church
20 Site of Horsemonger Lane Gaol
21 Joseph Lancaster School
22 Geoffrey Chaucer School

Based upon the Ordnance Survey mapping with permission of the Controller of Her Majesty's Stationery Office © Crown copyright. Unauthorised reproduction infringes Crown copyright and may lead to prosecution or civil proceedings. London Borough of Southwark. LA086541

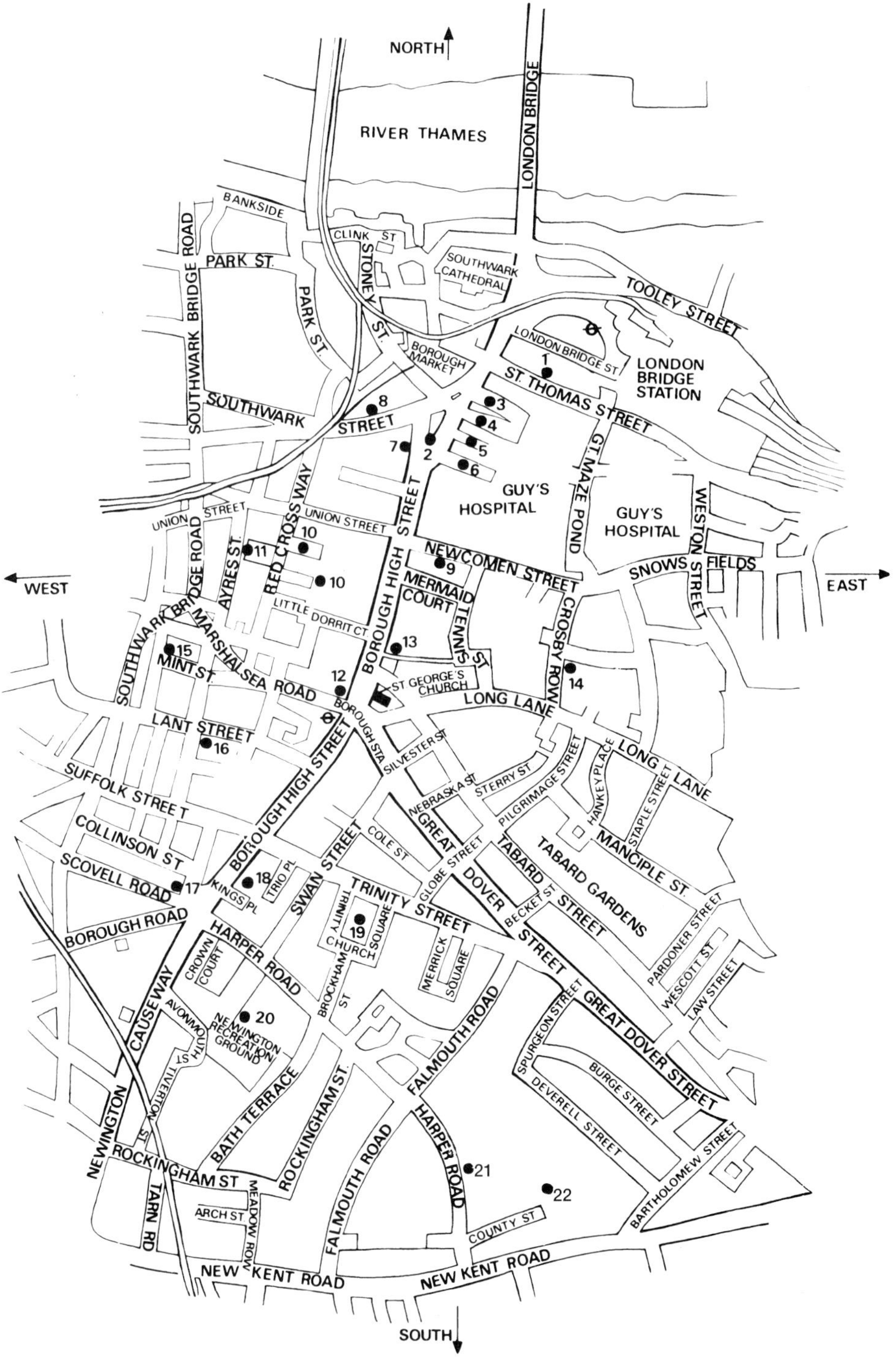
NORTH
RIVER THAMES
LONDON BRIDGE
BANKSIDE
CLINK ST
SOUTHWARK CATHEDRAL
TOOLEY STREET
SOUTHWARK BRIDGE ROAD
PARK ST.
PARK ST.
STONEY ST.
BOROUGH MARKET
LONDON BRIDGE ST
LONDON BRIDGE STATION
ST. THOMAS STREET
SOUTHWARK STREET
GT. MAZE POND
GUY'S HOSPITAL
GUY'S HOSPITAL
WESTON STREET
UNION STREET
UNION STREET
RED CROSS WAY
BOROUGH HIGH STREET
AYRES ST.
NEWCOMEN STREET
SNOWS FIELDS
WEST
EAST
MERMAID COURT
TENNIS ST
LITTLE DORRIT CT.
CROSBY ROW
SOUTHWARK BRIDGE ROAD
MARSHALSEA ROAD
MINT ST.
ST. GEORGE'S CHURCH
LONG LANE
BOROUGH STN.
LANT STREET
SILVESTER ST
LONG LANE
SUFFOLK STREET
NEBRASKA ST
STERRY ST
PILGRIMAGE STREET
HANKEY PLACE
STAPLE STREET
COLLINSON ST
BOROUGH HIGH STREET
COLE ST
GREAT DOVER STREET
GLOBE STREET
TABARD STREET
TABARD GARDENS
MANCIPLE ST.
SCOVELL ROAD
KINGS PL
TRIO PL
SWAN STREET
TRINITY STREET
TRINITY CHURCH SQUARE
BECKET ST
BOROUGH ROAD
HARPER ROAD
CROWN COURT
MERRICK SQUARE
BROCKHAM ST
PARDONER STREET
WESCOTT ST
LAW STREET
NEWINGTON CAUSEWAY
AVONMOUTH ST
NEWINGTON RECREATION GROUND
FALMOUTH ROAD
SPURGEON STREET
BURGE STREET
DEVERELL STREET
GREAT DOVER STREET
TIVERTON ST
BATH TERRACE
ROCKINGHAM ST.
HARPER ROAD
FALMOUTH ROAD
ROCKINGHAM ST
TARN RD
MEADOW ROW
ARCH ST.
COUNTY ST
BARTHOLOMEW STREET
NEW KENT ROAD
NEW KENT ROAD
SOUTH
1
2
3
4
5
6
7
8
9
10
10
11
12
13
14
15
16
17
18
19
20
21
22

Acknowledgments
The library would like to thank the Fine Art Society for permission to reproduce the illustration on the cover; Peter Froste for permission to reproduce the illustration inside the front cover and the Victoria and Albert Museum for permission to reproduce the illustration of the Tabard Inn.

London Borough of Southwark Neighbourhood Histories
1   The Story of Camberwell
2   The Story of Dulwich
3   The Story of Peckham
4   The Story of Walworth
5   The Story of Bermondsey
6   The Story of Rotherhithe
7   The Story of The Borough
8   The Story of Bankside

The Story of 'The Borough'

This booklet is a brief, simple introduction to the history of one part of the London Borough of Southwark. It is written mainly for younger readers who live or go to school in, or visit, the neighbourhood around Borough High Street, traditionally known as 'The Borough'. No.8 in the series covers Bankside and Blackfriars Road, the two parts overlap. Southwark Cathedral and London Bridge, important equally in the history of 'The Borough', are covered in No.8 and also some general topics for the whole area, such as industries and railways.

Some suggestions for further reading are given at the end of the book most of which are available at or through any Southwark library. Anyone wishing to make a more detailed study should visit the Local Studies Library, 211 Borough High Street, SE1 1JA. Tel: 0171 403 3507. This has a comprehensive collection of books, maps, illustrations, press cuttings, microfilms and archives covering all parts of the London Borough of Southwark. The opening hours may be obtained from any library. An appointment in advance is not necessary but it is advisable to book a microfilm reader in advance. School parties are welcome by prior arrangement.

Roman Southwark

Any weekday, Borough High Street, the road that leads to London Bridge, is jammed with cars, lorries and buses making their way to and from the City of London. How long has traffic of some kind been using this route? - Nearly two thousand years. Almost on the line of the modern street was a road built by the Romans, leading to a bridge and the Roman city of Londinium. Archaeologists have discovered various traces of it, most recently during the construction of the Jubilee Line.

In Roman times marching men, chariots, horses and carts were the traffic on the road. Part of a shoe worn by a Roman, or a Romano-Briton, who walked along this road, is now on show in the Cuming Museum, and the base of a standard carried by a standard-bearer of the Roman army was found in Stoney Street.

Borough High Street was the junction of two Roman highways which met near the present site of St George the Martyr Church. Old Kent Road and Tabard Street are on the line of Watling Street from Dover and the English Channel. Newington Causeway was part of Stane Street from Chichester and the Sussex coast.

When the Romans first arrived it was no easy task to build a road to the Thames crossing. The riverside was mostly mud and marshy ground, with various inlets from the river. In 1958 remains of a Roman boat were found where Guy's Hospital now stands. Some of the timbers are in the Cuming Museum. Borough High Street was built on the only stretch of firmer and higher ground, though even this was really three, separate, sandy islands. Skilled Roman road-builders bridged the gaps between them by first making ditches to drain the water away, then laying a foundation of timber logs, and on top of them putting a firm road surface. On the site of John Harvard Library archaeologists discovered the Roman road just to the east of the modern road, bridging what had been the water channel between two old islands.

A large Roman suburb grew up on either side of the road. Its history is everywhere buried beneath your feet. Whenever a building is demolished, archaeologists excavate and find evidence of Roman houses or objects the Romans used. Sometimes, for example at a large site in Southwark Street, they uncovered foundations of earlier buildings below later ones. Britain was part of the Roman empire for nearly 400 years and buildings were demolished and others erected on the site, just as now old houses are demolished for new developments. In fact people lived here even before Roman times. Below all the Roman remains was found evidence of what might have been an Iron Age Settlement.

Wealthy Romans lived in comfort and style. Bricks used for the hypocaust system of under-floor heating have been found and parts of the mosaic paving which covered these floors. Rooms were decorated with pictures and designs painted on the wall-plaster. Finds from excavations on show at the Cuming Museum include also pots and dishes of red Samian pottery from Gaul (France), large 'amphorae' or jars for wine, small pottery oil lamps, bone needles and hair pins. A green glass cup found near Tooley Street has pictures of gladiators fighting.

The most exciting discovery was in the crypt below Southwark Cathedral where, in 1977, archaeologists found a Roman well and in it several sculptures. One was a stone figure of a hunter god with a bow in his left hand and a dog by his side. Another was a marble dolphin, probably from a statue of Neptune, the sea-god. Why these objects were dumped in a well is a mystery. Perhaps, when Roman Britain became Christian, people wanted to be rid of their old gods.

Not much is known about Southwark immediately after the Romans left. Nature took over and perhaps crops were grown where once there had been fine buildings. A document written about 500 years later has the first known reference to 'the Borough of Southwark'.

Roman figure of a hunter god.
Found beneath Southwark Cathedral

'The Borough'

People who live in or around Borough High Street have good reason to say they live in 'the Borough'. Southwark was listed as a 'burgh', or borough, as early as 910AD in the Burghal Hideage, a list of 'burghs' with their 'hides', an old measurement of land. Of course a 'burgh' in those days meant something very different from a modern London Borough such as Southwark. It meant a stronghold, with fortifications to protect the river crossing. This was the original 'Southwark'. In the Burghal Hideage Southwark was spelt *Suthringa geweorche*, 'Surrey work', that is, the defence works of the people of Surrey. Later it was spelt *Sudwerca*, the South 'work' of the City of London.

Southwark is described in Domesday Book, the great survey of England compiled for William the Conqueror in 1086. It mentions a 'monasterium', a minster or large church, probably where Southwark Cathedral now stands, and various houses belonging to great Norman lords. By 1295 Southwark was important enough to have two Members of Parliament, the first district of London outside the City to be granted this right.

The oldest picture of 'the Borough' is part of *The Panorama of London* by Anthonis van den Wyngaerde c1544. It shows Borough High Street, sometimes called 'long Southwark', with buildings along both sides of it, and near the river a church which you would recognise as Southwark Cathedral. Its old name was the Priory of St Mary Overie. Later it was known as St Saviour's church and in 1905 it became a cathedral. In the foreground of a picture is the old St George the Martyr Church with a square tower, now replaced by a spire. Opposite the church is a grand palace, Suffolk Place, the home of Charles Brandon, Duke of Suffolk, whose wife Mary was a sister of King Henry VIII. Later the king took over the building and used it as a mint for making coins. The palace and mint have long disappeared but there is still a Mint Street and the new office building at the corner of Marshalsea Road has been named Brandon House.

If you look up Borough High Street from Brandon House you may just discern something of the old street pattern that Wyngaerde saw. Where the War Memorial now stands, there has always been

Southwark and London Bridge, based on a View of London *by Wyngaerde*

a triangular piece of ground between two roads - Borough High Street and Stoney Street. In the Middle Ages, St Margaret's Church stood on this triangle and part of Borough High Street was called St Margaret's Hill. Later the church was used as a courthouse and prison and later still a town hall was built on the site. Now a bank occupies the same piece of ground.

In Wyngaerde's time, behind the buildings along Borough High Street there was almost nothing but gardens and fields. Gradually all this open countryside was built over with crowded streets. Even in 1598 John Stow, the great historian of London, could write "The Borough of Southwark ... consisteth of divers streets, ways and winding lanes, all full of buildings. As a subsidy to the king, this borough yieldeth about ... eight hundred pounds, which is more than any one city in England payeth, except London."

The Borough inns

The sign of St George as a knight in armour hangs out over the pavement of Borough High Street. Go through the gateway beneath it and you seem to be in another world. The George Inn, with its galleries, looks like the inns of Shakespeare's day, except that then there would have been galleried buildings surrounding three sides of the inn-yard, instead of only one as today.

Once Borough High Street was lined with inns like this. Until 1750 London Bridge was the only bridge across the Thames at London and the street leading to it always had many travellers. At the Borough inns, they could get a drink, a meal, or a bed for the night, before setting out, or at the end of their journeys. The George, and many others, are marked on a map of 1542 and very clearly on the map of London made by John Rocque in 1746.

The most famous inn was the Tabard. In the Middle Ages pilgrims going to visit the shrine of St Thomas a Becket in Canterbury Cathedral gathered here before setting out on their journey. As poet Geoffrey Chaucer wrote in the *Prologue* to his *Canterbury Tales* -

> 'It happened in that season that one day
> In Southwark at the Tabard as I lay...
> At night there came into that hostelry
> Some nine and twenty in a company...
> That towards Canterbury meant to ride.
> The rooms and stables of the inn were wide.'
> (Modern English version by Nevill Coghill)

From the Tabard the pilgrims set off down 'Kent Street', now renamed Tabard Street, for the Old Kent Road to Canterbury.

The Tabard, like many of the inns, had to be rebuilt in 1676 after Southwark's own 'Great Fire', ten years after the Great Fire of London. The George was rebuilt then, so the present building is over 300 years old. Through the window to the bar you can see the oak beams of the ceiling and the big old fireplace.

In the 18th century the inns became more and more busy as coaches, horses and carriers' carts set off regularly from them for all parts of southern England. Services from the George included coaches four times a day to Maidstone, twice to Dover and Canterbury and daily to Brighton and Hastings. After leaving the inn-yards the horses' hooves would clatter over the cobblestones until they reached the Stones' End, where the police station now stands, and then, through the toll-gate, and out on to the turnpike road. The route to Kent, via narrow Kent Street, got so congested that in 1814 Great Dover Street was built as a by-pass.

Tabard Inn c. 1870

Charles Dickens knew the Borough inns. In his novel, *Pickwick Papers*, Mr Pickwick first met Sam Weller at the largest of them, the White Hart.

It was in 1836, when the railway came to Southwark, that the inns began to go out of business. People no longer travelled by horse-drawn coaches, but by train from London Bridge Station. All the inns were demolished, except the George, and of this two sides, and the stables, had gone before the National Trust took it over in 1937. Now it is the only inn of its kind left in London and tourists from all over the world come to visit it. Plays have sometimes been acted in the inn-yard as they were in the inn-yards of Shakespeare's day.

The other inns have gone, but not without trace. Leading off Borough High Street you see many narrow alleyways which were once entrances to inn-yards. Some have their names up - White Hart Yard, Talbot Yard (the later name of the Tabard) and Mermaid Court. In King's Head Yard there is a Victorian pub, but the sign over the door is a head of King Henry VIII, preserved from the old inn. In the Middle Ages this inn was the Pope's Head, but when Henry VIII quarrelled with the Pope the landlord must have renamed his inn! Another interesting sign is the royal coat of arms over the King's Arms, Newcomen Street, which was once over the gateway to Old London Bridge.

Between nos. 52 and 54 Borough High Street a little opening leads to what was once probably the Goat Inn, but is now known as Calvert's Buildings. This peaceful courtyard with its overhanging upper storey is a corner of very old Southwark which was not destroyed in the fire of 1676.

Southwark Fair and Borough Market

"From various parts, from various ends repair
A vast mix'd multitude to Southwark Fair."

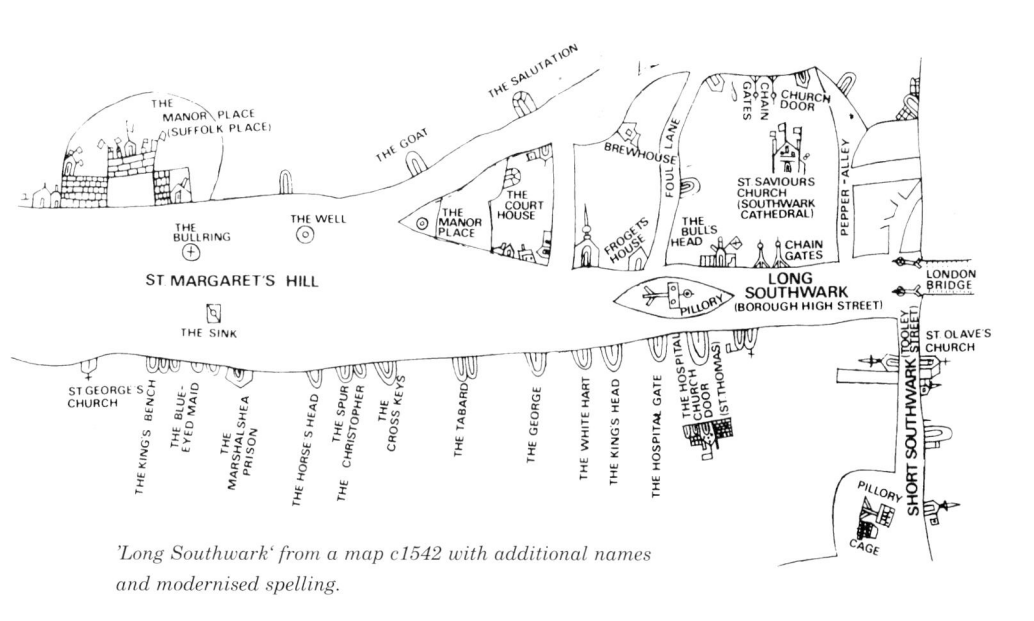

'Long Southwark' from a map c1542 with additional names and modernised spelling.

Every September for 300 years Borough High Street was a scene of great excitement, the annual Southwark Fair, in the Middle Ages sometimes known called 'St Margaret's Fair', from the nearby St Margaret's Church. The right to hold a Fair was granted to the City in 1462. Originally it lasted three days, but later fourteen.

There were all sorts of entertainments at the Fair. On the 21st September 1668 Samuel Pepys wrote in his famous diary "to Southwark Fair - and there saw a puppet show of (Dick) Whittington." He mentioned also that he left his purse with an inn-keeper for fear of pick-pockets! That other great diarist, John Evelyn, described a visit on 13th September 1660. "I saw in Southwark at St Margaret's Fair, monkeys and asses dance and do other feats on the tight rope'.

In 1733 the artist, William Hogarth, painted a picture of the Fair. In the centre is a drawing of a the Wooden Horse of Troy and a raised platform on which the story is being acted. A copy of the play *The Siege of Troy* 'presented ... in Southwark during the Fair' is in the Local Studies Library. In the background of Hogarth's picture is the old St George the Martyr Church, with a rope fixed to the top of the tower and a man sliding down it.

> *"So from the steeple Violante flies*
> *Loud shouts and acclamations rend the skies"*

Among other entertainments are a monkey with a hat on and a sword at his waist, and musicians with bagpipes, drums and trumpets. A poster advertises 'Maximilian, the Southwark Giant', said to have been ten and a half feet tall!

The Fair was held once a year but several days every week there was a busy street market in Borough High Street. It was one of the oldest markets in London with a history going back at least to 1276 and even earlier, when it was held on Old London Bridge.

Stalls were set up along both sides of the street from the Bridgefoot to St Margaret's Church; farmers with their bacon near the Bridge, then their wives selling butter, then the fishwives crying 'fresh fish from the Thames', then bakers, vegetable-sellers and butchers, who drove live animals to market. Ordinances of the market instructed them not to bring any oxen, bullocks or cows "that are soe wilde that they run awaie as often it happeneth". Farmers with sacks of flour could keep them dry in a market house near St Thomas' Street.

You can imagine the crowds, the noise and the lively scenes, but also the traffic jams, as horses, carts, coaches and carriages, tried to get through between the stalls on the main road to London. In 1756, due to congestion, the market was moved off the public highway and in 1762, for similar reasons, and because of rowdiness, Southwark Fair was held for the last time.

The market, however, did not come to an end. It moved to a piece of land known as the Triangle where it has become the famous Borough Market of today. Over the years its business completely changed. It became one of the great wholesale fruit and vegetable markets of London. Your local greengrocer may have gone there very early this morning to stock up his shop with produce from all over the world. It has a large covered Victorian market hall and a 20th century entrance and offices in Southwark Street. Unlike Covent Garden, the Borough Market stayed put in its old home. Many of the traders have fathers and grandfathers who had stalls there. Before 1756 the market was under the City of London when it then passed to the parishioners of St Saviour's.

Crime and Punishment

Old Southwark had more than its fair share of "felons, thieves, malefactors and disturbers of the peace". This was because, as the citizens of London complained to the King in 1327, criminals could flee across old London Bridge and the City Officers could not arrest them. Royal Charters were therefore issued granting the City rights over Southwark. In 1550 Southwark became 'The Bridge Ward Without', the ward (district) of the City of London 'without' (outside) the City Walls. There are still stones marking the boundaries of the City's authority. One is in the garden of Southwark Cathedral, facing Cathedral Street.

The Lord Mayor and Aldermen, or their officers, held courts to try offenders in the court-house on St Margaret's Hill. For example, dishonest traders at the Borough Market were punished. A butcher who sold bad meat might have to stand in the pillory while the smelly meat was burnt in front of him. The map of 1542 shows a pillory, with holes for head and arms, right in the middle of Borough High Street, and a second one in Tooley Street. Another old map shows the stocks and a 'cage' (small prison) south of the court-house. The City held a special court during Southwark Fair called the 'Court of Pie Powder', from the French 'pieds poudreux' meaning dusty feet. It was for people who had come to the Fair from outside Southwark, and had travelled along the unmade roads of those days.

In spite of efforts by the City, old Southwark still had some good hidey-holes for villains, the worst being the district known as 'The Mint', around Mint Street, which was then a maze of narrow streets and filthy alleys. It claimed to be a 'liberty' outside the authority of the City or any other power. It was the haunt of thieves such as two notorious highwaymen, Jack Sheppard and Jonathan Wild, both of whom were finally hanged at Tyburn. No wonder that the play, *The Beggars' Opera*, has a character called 'Matt of the Mint' as the leader of a gang of thieves.

The Mint was officially cleared of its debtors and criminals by an Act of Parliament in 1723 but, over 100 years later, Charles Dickens wrote of Lant Street "the population is migratory, usually disappearing on the verge of quarter-day (when the rent was due!) and generally by night." When the district was rebuilt, the streets were given names from Dickens' novels, such as Weller Street, Copperfield Street, and Little Dorrit Court.

Old prisons

"Five jails, or prisons are in Southwark placed
The Counter once St Margaret's Church defaced
The Marshalsea, the King's Bench and White Lyon,
Then there's the Clink where handsome lodgings be."

John Taylor 1630

Except for the Clink, in Clink Street, all these grim prisons were in Borough High Street, next door to the famous inns, overlooking the market and fair. Why were there so many? The Counter or Borough Compter was for those convicted at the court-house "once St Margaret's Church". The other prisons were not just for local criminals. They were probably placed in Southwark because it was near to London but outside the City walls. The King's Bench and the Marshalsea were royal prisons. The White Lyon, which had earlier been an inn, was a jail for the County of Surrey.

Prisoners in all the prisons suffered terribly and many died of the dreaded jail fever brought on by overcrowding and unhealthy conditions. A prisoner in the King's Bench wrote "As to health, it hath more diseases in it than the pest-house in the plague-time ... it stinks more than the Lord Mayor's dog-house". Prisoners could die of starvation as they were expected to beg their food from passers-by. They might also suffer torture.

Not all prisoners were criminals. Unhappily, even today, in some countries there are "prisoners of conscience". So it was in England in the 16th and 17th centuries. Brave Christians, sometimes Protestants and sometimes Roman Catholics, were put in prison because their religious beliefs differed from those in power.

Many people were in prison simply because they had got into debt and, unless they had wealthy friends, might well stay there for the rest of their lives. Charles Dickens' father was imprisoned in the Marshalsea, fortunately for only a short time. While he was there, young Charles had lodgings in Lant Street, near where Charles Dickens School is today.

Dickens also knew the Horsemonger Lane Gaol in what is now Harper Road. On the roof were gallows where, in 1849, Mr and Mrs Manning from Bermondsey were publicly hanged

Horsemonger Lane Gaol

for the murder of their lodger. It was a horrifying crime but, as Dickens wrote in a famous letter to *The Times* newspaper, even more horrifying was the behaviour of the crowds who gathered to watch. Twenty years later public executions were abolished in England.

Fortunately all these old prisons have long since been demolished. The site of the Horsemonger Lane Gaol was made into the Newington Gardens Recreation Ground which some old people still call 'the gaol playground'. Next to the playground is the Crown Court in Newington Causeway. The King's (or Queen's) Bench, earlier on the east side of Borough High Street, was moved in 1758 to the corner of Borough Road. It was replaced by Victorian blocks of flats known as Queen's Buildings but they too have made way for the new Scovell housing estate. Counter Court, between Borough High Street and Southwark Street, marks the site of the Counter Prison. All that is left of any of the old prisons is one high brick wall of the Marshalsea. It overshadows the alley leading to the Local Studies Library. An old pump from the Marshalsea is in the Cuming Museum.

Two great hospitals

Until 1862, two great hospitals, St Thomas' and Guy's, faced each other across St Thomas' Street, just off Borough High Street. Guy's is still there. St Thomas' has moved to the Lambeth riverside.

St Thomas' was founded about 800 years ago by the Priory of St Mary Overie. Over the years it grew into a large hospital stretching the length of St Thomas' Street, with a church for the people of St Thomas' parish. Among these in the 16th century were famous craftsmen, who made stained glass windows for King's College, Cambridge and printed the first Bible in English to be printed in England.

Three centuries later it was at St Thomas' Hospital that modern nursing began. In earlier times nurses were untrained and often rough or even drunk. After the Crimean War, Florence Nightingale founded here the 'Nightingale School', the first training school for nurses in the world.

Eventually St Thomas' had to move to make way for an extension to London Bridge Station. Its buildings were demolished except for one block, which is now occupied by the post office in Borough High Street. The church, a fine building of Queen Anne's reign, also survives and but is now used for other purposes. Next to the church is a wide gateway, once the side entrance to the hospital, and houses which were the homes of officials such as the treasurer and the apothecary (chemist).

But climb the stairs in the church tower and a surprise awaits you. Here is an old operating theatre of the hospital, only rediscovered in 1956. It has a narrow wooden table where surgeons performed operations, without anaesthetics. Underneath there is a box of sawdust to catch the blood! Also in the roof is the Herb Garret where the apothecary stored and mixed herbs for medicine.

Guy's Hospital, front quadrangle, c 1890

St Thomas' Hospital, c1861

Guy's Hospital was founded in 1726 by Thomas Guy, the son of a river boatman, of Fair Street, Bermondsey. Guy made a fortune, largely through clever investments, and became a Governor of St Thomas'. When he saw that this hospital, large as it was, could not take in all the patients needing care - especially those considered to be incurable - he decided to use much of his fortune to build another hospital across the road. In his will he left £220,000 to maintain 'Guy's Hospital'.

The Latin motto over the entrance reads "Dare quam accipere", "(it is more blessed) to give than to receive". The statue of Guy, by the sculptor Peter Scheemakers, stands in the centre of the oldest part of the hospital. The hospital grew, thanks to many later benefactors, for example William Morris, Lord Nuffield, the man who started Morris Motors. His statue is in an inner courtyard.

Behind the fairly low old buildings rises the 11-storey New Guy's House opened in 1961, and the 30-storey Guy's Tower opened in 1975. Floors 9-12 of this are the Evelina Children's Department which replaces the Evelina Children's Hospital, Southwark Bridge Road, demolished 1975. Guy's now has beds for about 1,000 patients and, in the training of doctors and nurses, is one of the great teaching hospitals of the world.

John Keats, the poet, was a medical student at Guy's.

St George the Martyr church and parish

Look up from Borough High Street, Newington Causeway, Long Lane, Great Dover Street or Tabard Street and you will see, standing out from the modern developments, the spire of St George the Martyr. There has been a church at this road junction since at least 1122, when the right to appoint the rector was given to Bermondsey Abbey.

The church was rebuilt in 1736 by the architect John Price. As you go in, notice the columns, like those of a Greek temple, on either side of the entrance, and the carvings of angels above it. Over the years the people of St George the Martyr have cared for their church and added to its beauty. Sit down in one of the old pews and look up. The ceiling was designed by Basil Champneys in 1897 and renewed after war-time damage. It shows the Glory of God breaking through the clouds. The words are from two hymns of praise - the *Te Deum* "We praise thee O God" and the *Benedicite* "All ye works of the Lord, bless ye the Lord".

The bells and the organ are from the older church and some stones from it are on show in the crypt. The font is a copy of the old one. There are Registers from 1602 to the present day of all the babies christened in the church and also of people married or buried there. On the walls are memorials to people who lived in the parish. The small open space across Tabard Street was once part of the Burial Ground.

People call St George the Martyr "Little Dorrit's church". According to the novel by Charles Dickens, Little Dorrit lived with her father in Marshalsea Prison just north of the church, where Dickens' own father had once been imprisoned. One night, on returning home too late, Little Dorrit slept in the church vestry using one of the old registers as a pillow. The modern east window has a small picture of Little Dorrit.

St George the Martyr Church, c1925

St George the Martyr was once the church for a large parish stretching south down Old Kent Road nearly to Albany Road and west to what is now the Imperial War Museum. Its northern boundary was Newcomen Street where there is a parish boundary mark with the letters St. G.M. The people who lived north of this street were in St Saviour's parish.

St George the Martyr, like other parishes, had its own local government. The Churchwardens had many duties. In 1738, long before everyone could get water from a tap, they decided to pay £1 a year to have water piped from the Thames at Dockhead. It was stored in the old lead cistern which is now placed in the church near the font. A Committee known as the Vestry governed the parish, meeting round the oak table which is still in the church vestry. The Vestry Minutes from 1716 are in Southwark Local Studies Library. In 1868 the Vestry decided to have the church clock lit by gas lighting but, to save money, they only lit up three of the four faces. One clock face is still black, although the clock is now lit by electricity.

John Harvard

No. 211 Borough High Street, part of one of the modern buildings in the street, houses the John Harvard Library. The busy lending department provides for readers, young and old, who live and work in the neighbourhood. Behind it is the separate Local Studies Library where you can study material on the history of the whole London Borough of Southwark. The name John Harvard is a reminder of a famous son of the Borough and one well suited to have its library named after him.

Born in 1607, John Harvard was christened at St Saviour's Church, now Southwark Cathedral, and attended St Saviour's Grammar School, before going to Cambridge University. His father was a well-to-do Borough High Street butcher and also owned one of the famous inns, the Queen's Head.

Harvard lived in a great period in Southwark's history, when Shakespeare's plays were having their first productions at the Globe Theatre on Bankside. But he also lived at a sad time. Like so many other families he lost nearly all his close relations - his father and four of his brothers and sisters - in an outbreak of the plague in 1625. John was left with all the family fortune but no wonder, perhaps, that he and his wife, Ann, decided to leave Southwark and start a new life in America, where the first colonies were just being founded. They arrived in Boston on 26th June 1637 and took a house near Charlestown. John soon became a member of the Committee which was making laws for the Colony.

Sadly he died only a year later, not yet 31, but his Will benefited his 'New England' home right down to the present day. As it says in the records "It pleased God to stir up the heart of Mr Harvard, a godly gentleman and lover of learning, to give one half of his Estate towards the erecting of a college, and all his library". This gift was so important that the college, which was founded in Cambridge, Massachusetts, was named Harvard. It grew into the great Harvard University, the equal in America of Cambridge or Oxford in England. John Harvard's library was also of much value. This young tradesman's son from Southwark had brought with him across the Atlantic, over 400 volumes, including books on religion, works in Latin and Greek, grammar books which he used at St Saviour's School, and even a copy of Aesop's Fables which he probably enjoyed as a child.

Harvard University has not forgotten its Southwark benefactor. A chapel in Southwark Cathedral has been restored "by the sons and friends of Harvard University" and named in his memory the Harvard Chapel. John Harvard Library was officially opened in 1977 by the American Cultural Attaché. Southwark is certainly proud to have been the birthplace of John Harvard.

Documentaries

You must often have seen TV 'documentaries' - programmes based on real life. In the Local Studies Library there are documents, or archives, of St George the Martyr and other parishes, which could suggest hundreds of 'documentaries', though they may need scholars to transcribe the old handwriting.

Can you picture, for example, the suffering of people during the outbreak of the Plague? Southwark was 'visited' by this dreaded disease not only in 1665, the year of the Great Plague of London, but also in 1625 and 1636 and other years. One of the oldest archives is a notebook entitled "The account of money for the use of the parishioners of St George the Martyr visited by the plague 1636-37". Addresses include the Mint, Long Lane and Kent Street.

Many of the archives are concerned with the 'Poor Law'. Before there was any National Insurance, householders had to pay Poor Rates to help the old, sick and unemployed in their own parish. Ratebooks for St George the Martyr, listing names and addresses of ratepayers, go back to the 17th century.

Many 'Poor Law' documents show the sadder side of life in the past. For example the Workhouse Minutes give the 'Bill of fare' for St George the Martyr Workhouse, in 1729. Some days of the week the poor inmates had just porridge or broth for both breakfast and dinner. Some people think that Dickens was picturing this workhouse when he wrote Oliver Twist. Fortunately, all that is left of it are some of the walls around the Mint Street Adventure Playground.

Poor children, like Oliver, were apprenticed to learn a trade. Some were sent all the way to the cotton and wool mills of northern England. A letter of about 1780 addressed to St George the Martyr from a firm in Cheshire, sets out a "plan for disposing of 200 parish children". It says "we take them at 9 or 10 years old... they labour from 6am to 7pm in summer and from 7am to 8pm in winter. In the evening after work they wash, get their suppers and go to school, from thence to bed."

The Library has many apprenticeship documents, or 'indentures'. One reads "Ann Blake, aged ten years, a poor child, apprentice to Jonas Whitaker of Burley in the County of York, calico weavers, with him to dwell and serve - until she shall accomplish her full age of 21 years". Ann received no wages but her master promised "sufficient meat, drink and apparel (clothes), lodgings and washing."

When poor people from other parts of the country came to Southwark, probably looking for work, they were often sent back as ratepayers did not want to pay out 'poor relief' for people not born or legally settled in their parish. What story lies behind this 'removal order' of St George the Martyr parish, dated 14th December, 1743? "To remove Judith Burnell, wife of John Burnell, now abroad, and her two children, Mary aged four and Anthony about one year, to the village of Alkington in Gloucester, where they were last legally settled".

'Fire Rewards' are a different type of document. On 27th April, 1781 one James Stretton was awarded twenty shillings (£1) because "he brought to a fire at the workshop of Mr Fowler in Kent Street, the engine belonging to the Sun Fire Office in good order with a suction hose, leather pipe and stand cock". There was no London Fire Brigade in those days. Horse drawn fire engines raced to the fire to win the reward. Over the office of Field and Son, Borough High Street, there is still the trademark of the Sun Fire Insurance Company.

A place to live

'The Borough' is certainly rich in history, but it is also a place where people live. The oldest and most beautiful houses are in the Trinity Church Square Conservation Area. Those around the Square with Trinity Street and Falmouth Road were built about 1831 and Merrick Square about 1856. They look almost as when the first residents moved in, arriving probably by carriage and horse. Even the electric street lights are copies of old gas lamps.

The estate, in the old parish of St Mary Newington, belongs to Trinity House to whom the land was given in 1661, by Christopher Merrick, 'for relieving poor, aged, sick seamen of this country'. Notice the Trinity House coat of arms of four sailing ships, on a wall in Trinity Street.

In the centre of Trinity Church Square is the former Holy Trinity Church, designed by the architect, Francis Bedford. It was restored after war-time damage and is now used by London orchestras for rehearsals. Its new name is the Henry Wood Hall, after the famous conductor. The statue in the garden, said to be King Alfred, is probably from Westminster Hall and about 600 years old.

Trinity Church Square, 1830

Not everyone lived in such fine houses as Trinity Church Square. When they were built the area was becoming one of the poorest and most crowded in London. Today only about 8,000 people live in the old parish of St George the Martyr, but in 1851 there were over 51,000 and in 1901 over 60,000. As a Medical Officer of Health wrote in 1858, "Overcrowding is the normal state of our poorer districts. Small houses of four rooms are usually inhabited by three or four families and by 8, 16 or 24 persons". Maypole Alley, where Maypole House now stands, was described as "a nest of infectious diseases".

Gradually the old slums were swept away. Marshalsea Road was opened up across the Mint district and the blocks of flats now under the Peabody Trust were built by the Improved Industrial Dwellings Company. Over Douglas Buildings is the date 1886. Families who moved in over a hundred years ago were no doubt pleased to find, perhaps for the first time in their lives, sinks with running water, proper drains and toilets - things we now take for granted.

Tabard Street was another area of overcrowded courts and alleys. It was here that the Charterhouse Mission was founded in 1884 by old boys of Charterhouse School. The Mission Church, St Hugh's, was dedicated in 1898. Charterhouse-in-Southwark continues its good work today but in very different surroundings. In 1887 the Metropolitan Board of Works began clearing the slums, which were later replaced by blocks of flats and an open space - Tabard Gardens.

Most people in north Southwark now live in blocks of flats, built either by the London County Council, later the Greater London Council, or by Southwark Borough Council. Octavia Hill, a lady who did much to improve London's housing, had other ideas. She planned the pretty cottages in Redcross Way, Ayres Street and Sudrey Street on land belonging to the Church Commissioners. Thanks to her efforts also Redcross Gardens were laid out, where previously there had been only a rubbish dump. Notice the mosaic picture of the 'Sower' erected by Octavia Hill in 1896.

Some of the newest housing is the Scovell Estate built by the London Borough of Southwark in 1978. Like the Octavia Hill cottages it consists of individual houses, two storeys high, and seems almost like a village in the midst of London.

Schools, old and new

The children of the Cathedral School of St Saviour and St Mary Overie go to new school buildings, but to the oldest school still in North Southwark. Like other 'parish' or 'charity' schools, it was founded long before there was any state education. In 1681 Mrs Dorothy Applebee gave £20 for a 'free' school in St Saviour's parish. It was originally in the churchyard, later in Union Street and, since 1977, in Redcross Way. Next to it is St Joseph's, the Roman Catholic Church School. St George the Martyr Parish Schools, founded in 1698, have amalgamated with St Jude's School, Colnbrook Street.

Mrs Elizabeth Newcomen, who lived about the same time as Mrs Applebee, left houses to provide education and clothes for boys and girls. You can still find her property mark 'Mrs N' on buildings in Newcomen Street. The Elizabeth Newcomen School closed in 1970. Elizabeth Newcomen's and other old charities are still used to help young people.

Joseph Lancaster School, Harper Road, is named after a local man who became famous for schools that he founded. He lived in Kent Street, which was then a very crowded neighbourhood, with hundreds of poor children who had no chance of learning to read and write. He started his first school in 1798 in Borough Road. As he did not have enough money to pay assistant teachers, he used 'monitors', older boys and girls, to teach the younger ones. He said that in this way one master could manage 1,000 children! To save buying books they had pages of the Bible in large print hanging on the walls and repeated their lessons by heart. They wrote on slates.

Schools following the 'Monitorial' system were soon opening all over England, and in other countries, and monitors came to Joseph Lancaster's school for training. In 1818 a black boy, William Jagon, was monitor-general. He later became Master of a school in the West Indies. To carry on the work the British and Foreign Schools' Society was founded and built a Teachers' Training College in Borough Road. In 1890 the building was taken over by the Borough Polytechnic, now part of the huge South Bank University.

St Saviour's Grammar School for Boys, 1815

After 1870 the State began providing schools. Those in Southwark came under the London School Board. According to the plaque in Toulmin Street, Charles Dickens School was once the Lant Street Board School, built in 1877. Compare the architecture of this 'Board School' with Geoffrey Chaucer School, built in 1961.

The small statue of Elizabeth I on the outside of St Saviour's and St Olave's Girls' School, New Kent Road, opened in 1903, is a reminder of the oldest schools in North Southwark of which there are records. Grammar schools for St Saviour's parish and St Olave's, Tooley Street, were both founded over 400 years ago in Queen Elizabeth I's reign. The boys' school moved to Orpington in 1968.

Shops and trade

About 300 years ago Mr Nicholas Hare, with his son William, had a grocer's shop in Borough High Street. Their shop sign, a hare and the sun, is now in the Cuming Museum.

For centuries, Borough High Street was a shopping street. The oldest shops and houses had narrow fronts, just enough for a front door and windows on the street, but with plenty of room behind for buildings and back gardens. These long narrow building sites, some still existing today, are known as 'burgage plots', plots of land in a borough.

In Victorian times Borough High Street was especially busy and prosperous. In 1831 old London Bridge had been replaced by a new bridge, a little to the west, and the northern part of the street was re-aligned and widened. New roads already linked it with Blackfriars Road and the rest of London, the first being Borough Road, opened in 1751. Union Street, opened in 1781, still has a few old shopfronts - for example nos. 59-61. Southwark Street, opened in 1864, has some grand Victorian warehouses and office buildings.

Shoppers for fashionable clothes or furniture came to 'the Borough' from other parts by horse-bus or by train to London Bridge. Old tradesmen's advertisements show what the shops were like; Brooks & Co. at nos 145-149 was a magnificent looking store with ladies arriving by carriage to buy their 'shawls and mantles'. William Tarn & Co., Newington Causeway and New Kent Road, had their own workshops for reproducing "the latest Paris fashions". All these grand stores have now gone. Above the modern shopfronts you can still see the Victorian facades and sometimes the old names.

The 'Borough' was not only shops; it was also a place where things were made. Kent Street was described in 1720 as "chiefly inhabited by broom men" who had yards with "vast stocks of birch and broom staves". No vacuum cleaners in those days!

The Hop and Malt Exchange building, Southwark Street, Borough

Brandon House is built on the site of Nettlefold and Moser's, an ironmonger's business handed down over 100 years in the Moser family. When all road traffic was horse-drawn they had a factory which could turn out five tons of horse-shoe nails weekly. There were many such family firms. Smith Kendon Ltd. were making sweets in 128 Borough High Street for over 100 years until 1974. Stevenson's ironmongers was a name in 'the Borough' for over a century. Probably the oldest business still in the family is Field & Son. The present Mr Field is the seventh generation in a firm of estate agents established in 1804.

The 'Borough' was especially noted as the centre of the English hop-trade. Sacks of hops, or hop pockets, were brought from Kent, Worcester and Hereford and from abroad to be stored in the hop merchants' warehouses and then sold to brewers for making beer, notably Barclay Perkins in Park Street and Courage's on the Bermondsey riverside. Old cranes which lifted hop sacks or other goods may be seen high up outside some old buildings - for example in Chapel Yard, Union Street.

In 1866 a magnificent Hop and Malt Exchange was erected in Southwark Street. Like all hop buildings it had a glass roof so that the quality of hops could be examined by good natural lighting. It is now used for offices; but notice the stone carving of hop-pickers over the entrance and the hops in the ironwork of the gates.

The hop-trade left 'the Borough' in about 1970, when brewers began using hop essence and hop pellets instead of raw hops. The hop factors and brewers have moved out of Southwark and hop-picking itself has been mechanised. Only older people can now remember going hopping in the fields of Kent.

Two World Wars

In the centre of Borough High Street, opposite the George Inn, is a bronze figure of a soldier. It is a memorial to the 334 men of St Saviour's Parish who gave their lives in World War I, 1914-1918. The inscription reads "May their memory live for ever in the minds of men", but traffic hurries by without noticing. Walk round the memorial and look at the pictures on the stone base of Great War ships, guns and aeroplanes. In the *South London Press* of the time are stories of some of the heroes, for example - Corporal Henry Cross of Mermaid Court, who won the Victoria Cross for recapturing, single-handed, two machine guns which had fallen into enemy hands.

In World War II, 1939-1945, everyone was involved. 925 civilians died in the old Metropolitan Borough of Southwark, many of them in 'the Borough' area. The printed list of Civilian War Dead gives their names and addresses. 16th October 1940, was a terrible night when crowded Queen's Buildings, Scovell Road, got a direct hit, and even those who had taken refuge in the air-raid shelters did not escape as a water-main burst and flooded them.

There was only one safe, deep shelter; the disused section of an old underground line - the City and South London Railway. In 1900 the line north of Borough Station had been rebuilt on a slightly different route, that now taken by the Northern Line, and the disused section had been sealed up. It was reopened in 1940 as an air-raid shelter for up to 8,000 people. A concrete floor covered the old railway tracks and at first people slept on it, propped up against the walls. Later bunk beds were installed with numbers so that regular shelterers could come back night after night to their own bunks. Six entrances were made so people could get down quickly when the siren sounded. One was in Union Street playground and another in the Garden of St George the Martyr. All have now been filled in.

When people came out of the shelters they might find their homes in ruins and have to go to a 'Rest Centre'. Charles Dickens School was used for this purpose.

The St Saviour's War Memorial at its unveiling in 1922

Guy's Hospital suffered badly in the Blitz of 1940-41, being hit by high explosive and incendiary bombs. Yet the healing work of the hospital never stopped. During the war years, in addition to ordinary patients, 3,089 air-raid injuries were treated by the doctors and nurses of Guy's.

A Borough panorama

If film or video could have recorded 'the Borough' for the past 2,000 years, you would have a panorama of all periods of English history, with commentary from some of them by such great names as Chaucer, Stow, Pepys and Dickens.

Just as TV news often seems to concentrate on wars and riots rather than on peaceful days, so you might particularly notice such events in pictures of 'the Borough". In 1066 all of its buildings were set on fire by William the Conqueror as he advanced towards London after winning the Battle of Hastings. In 1381 Wat Tyler, leading the Peasants' Revolt, was joined by men of Southwark and broke open the Marshalsea Prison before crossing into the City. In 1450 another rebel, Jack Cade, and his followers, made the White Hart their headquarters. During the Civil War between 'Cavaliers' and 'Roundheads' one of the ring of forts built by Parliament to defend London was near the site of the Borough High Street police station. In the 17th century Southwark, like the City, suffered from plague and fire and in the 20th century from two world wars.

Royal occasions bring happier pictures. Many kings and queens have come this way: Henry V after his victory at Agincourt and Charles II returning from exile. Borough High Street was splendidly decorated for Queen Victoria's Diamond Jubilee in 1897. George VI and Queen Elizabeth, now the Queen Mother, made a visit during the worst period of the war.

These are just a few of the newsworthy events, but all the while the ordinary busy life of 'the Borough' went on. Some aspects of it were bad, its prisons and its poverty, many good, its inns, market and fair, hospitals, trade and industry; and two great churches, St Saviour's and St George the Martyr. Over the centuries this neighbourhood has been in turn a suburb of Roman London, an Anglo-Saxon burgh, a market town, a travellers' meeting-point at the gateway to London Bridge and a crowded 'inner city' area of Victorian London. In 1900 it became part of the Metropolitan Borough of Southwark and, in 1965, of the London Borough of Southwark.

In the lifetime of older people much that they remember seems to have gone. Industry and trade have largely moved out. With a smaller population and easier transport to the West End, Borough High Street is no longer an important shopping street. Its few shops are small grocers, and chemists for local needs. Many old buildings have been demolished and office blocks of big national and international companies tend to replace them.

At the same time, people realise that the Borough High Street is a street of history. The neighbourhood has been made a Conservation Area. Redevelopment is going on behind Borough High Street and St Thomas' Street but it is well hidden by old buildings which have now been listed. There are many 'listed' buildings also in Newcomen Street, Southwark Street, Stoney Street, Union Street and Trinity Church Square.

Visitors find this part of Southwark a fascinating place. They come mainly to see the 'Little Dorrit Church', the George Inn, Southwark Cathedral, and nearby Bankside. But if you live here, or have more time, you can enjoy discovering the less obvious survivals from the past and getting to know the whole character of the neighbourhood.

So now go out and explore every inch of it, and then come back to the Local Studies Library, right in the heart of it, where you can begin a real study of 'The Story of the Borough'.

Booklist

Dillon, J. *Archaeology in Southwark Investigation results 1990-1*, LBS 1992

Dillon, J. *Archaeology in Southwark Investigation results 1993*, LBS 1994

Dillon, J. *Archaeology in Southwark Investigation results 1994*, LBS 1995

Museum of London Archaeology Service, *Annual Report,* 1996.

Rendle, W. *Old Southwark and its people,* Longmans 1878.

Carlin, M. *Medieval Southwark;* Hambledon Press, 1996.

Johnson, D. *Southwark and the City,* Corporation of London 1969.

Rendle, W. *Inns of Old Southwark and their associations,* Longmans, 1888.

Prettejohns, G and others. *Charles Dickens and Southwark,* LBS 1994.

An illustrated History of Borough Market, The Trustees, c1995.

McInnes, EM. *St Thomas' Hospital,* Allen Unwin, 1963.

Ripmar, RA. *Guy's Hospital,* Guy's Hospital Gazette, 1951.

Pinder, J. *St George the Martyr,* The church, 1965.

Rundell, D and Tichelor, M. *Class Struggle in South London*, Southwark and Lambeth History Workshop, 1980.

Carrington, RC. *Two Schools,* St. Olave's School, 1971.

Bartle, GF. *A history of Borough Road College,* the College, 1976.

Davis, Rib ed. *Southwark at war,* LBS, 1996.

Bancroft, P. *The Railway to King William Street,* Author, 1981.

Culpin, Chris. *Victorian Southwark. A local history pack,* LBS, 1997.

Darlington, Ida. *Survey of London Vol XXV St George's Fields,* LCC, 1955.

Godfrey, Walter. *Survey of London Vol XXII Bankside,* LCC, 1950.

Van den Wyngaerde, Anthonis, *The Panorama of London circa 1544,* London Topographical Society, 1996

Index

Bedford, Francis	23	Markets see: Borough Market	
Bridge Ward Without	10	Marshalsea Prison	12, 13
Borough High Street	1, 8, 20, 27	Marshalsea Road	24, 32
		Mint	3, 11
Borough Market	9, 10		
Borough Polytechnic	25	Poor Law	21-22
Broom manufacture	27	Price, John	17
Burghal Hideage	3	Prisons	10-13
Charterhouse in Southwark	24	Newcomen Street	25
Clink Prison	12	Octavia Hill	24
Criminals	10		
		Railways	7
Dickens, Charles	7, 11, 12, 17	Roman period	1-2
Domesday book	3		
		St George the Martyr Church	1, 3, 9, 17-19, 30
Fairs	8		
Field & Son, estate agents	29	St Margaret's Church	4, 8, 9
		St Mary Overie Priory	3, 14
Guy's Hospital	1, 14, 16, 31	St Saviour's Church	3
		St Saviour's and St Olave's School	26
Harvard, John	20-21		
Holy Trinity Church	23-24	St Thomas' Church	14
Hop Trade	29	St Thomas' Hospital	14
Horsemonger Lane Gaol	12	Schools	25-26
Hospitals see: St Thomas' Hospital and Guy's Hospital		Shops	27-28, 33
		Southwark Cathedral see also: St Saviour's Church	2, 10, 21
Industry	29	Southwark Street	2, 27
Inns	5-7	South Bank University	25
		Suffolk Place	3
Joseph Lancaster School	25		
		Tabard Inn	5, 6, 7
King's Bench Prison	12	Tabard Street	5
		Trinity Church Square	23-24, 33
Lancaster, Joseph	25		
London Bridge	5, 7, 9, 27		
London, City of	10	Wars	30-1
London School Board	26	White Lyon prison	12

Contents

Series Editor's note	**VIII**
Preface	**IX**
Chapter 1 Verbal protocol analysis	**1**
Introduction	1
What is verbal protocol analysis?	1
The different categories of verbal protocols	4
Theoretical background	7
Validity and reliability of verbal reports	10
Some applications for verbal protocol analysis	13
The procedure for carrying out VPA	14
What are the disadvantages in using verbal protocols?	20
A range of validation questions	21
Summary	30
Chapter 2 Data preparation and collection	**31**
Introduction	31
Task identification	35
Task analysis	38
Procedure selection	40
Using supplementary data	40
Data collection	41
Data transcription	50
Worked examples	52
Summary	66
Tutorial exercise	67
Chapter 3 Developing a coding scheme	**68**
Introduction	68
Developing a coding scheme	69
Example	71
Identifying the main unit for analysis	73
Segmenting the protocols	75
Worked examples	78

Summary	91
Tutorial exercise	91

Chapter 4 Analysing verbal protocol data — **92**
Introduction	92
Coding the protocols	92
Establishing the reliability of codings	92
Data analysis techniques	94
Worked examples	103
Summary	116
Tutorial exercise	116

Chapter 5 Overview and future directions — **117**

References	**121**
Appendices	**125**
Subject Index	**170**
Author Index	**174**

Series Editor's note

Thinking on the place of validation in language testing has evolved in the last decade with much more emphasis being placed on qualitative methods. These are being used increasingly to complement the quantitative approaches widely used in the eighties. This volume focuses on verbal protocol analysis, a technique used fairly extensively in the validation of Cambridge examinations and elsewhere in recent years. In Cambridge we first used the approach to better inform us of what raters attended to in the marking of essays in order to improve the effectiveness of subjective assessment. The work is extensively discussed in this volume.

During the project we became aware that, although there was a relatively extensive literature on protocol analysis, there was no single source which took an in-depth view of how the approach could be applied to issues in language testing, nor indeed how to go about the practical tasks of data preparation and capture, developing coding schemes or analysing verbal protocol data with worked examples directly relevant to language testers.

Given this situation I decided to commission a volume with the express purpose of providing language testers with a comprehensive account of the issues involved and practical implications of verbal protocol analysis to language testing. This approach was taken because it provides readers with important insights into how verbal protocol analysis can be used effectively and the areas in which verbal protocol analysis can be most usefully applied. Such areas include the testing of reading, writing, listening and speaking, the selection and edition of material, its trialling, pretesting and the evaluation of pretested materials. There is no doubt that the methodology is difficult to work with and very time consuming to carry out. Nevertheless, I am convinced that the approach merits more attention and that it can help us gain a deeper understanding of what we are doing and why.

The validation theme will run through a number of forthcoming volumes in this series. We are currently working on a handbook which will focus on the use of qualitative analysis when working with oral interview data, an approach that draws heavily on work in conversation analysis. We are also working on a handbook which further explores the use of structural modelling in the investigation of the relationships between test-taker characteristics and test performance which develops further the work carried out by Anthony Kunnan in Volume 2 of this series.

Michael Milanovic
Cambridge, July 1997

Preface

The methodology of verbal protocol analysis is one introspective technique that is being used increasingly for a wide range of applications. This book concerns itself with the use of verbal protocol analysis in language testing. The term 'language testing' is used broadly, for the book does not seek simply to describe the ways in which verbal protocol analysis may be used in the field of second language testing. Instead, it sets out to show that the technique may be used in the fields of both first and second language use, and in second language acquisition. Issues in acquiring a first language are not a central concern here.

Validity and reliability are two related and crucial terms in the field of assessment. Validity centres on what the assessment instrument measures, whereas reliability concerns itself with the accuracy and stability of judgements made about the skill or ability in question. An instrument may be reliable but not valid, but cannot be valid if it is not reliable. For our purposes, the validation process includes procedures that serve to establish validity and to estimate reliability.

The range of tasks used to consider issues in language testing include:

- writing in both the first and the second language,
- reading,
- listening,
- translation, and
- speaking.

The source of data is not always the test taker. In order to answer some of the validation questions that arise as part of the test development process, it is sometimes necessary to switch our attention to the examiner. Thus, the examples that are described in this book use excerpts from verbal reports generated by both students and examiners.

First, some words on terminology are required. Frequently, the terms verbal protocol analysis, protocol analysis, discourse analysis, verbal reports, verbal data, and introspection are used. Verbal protocol analysis, protocol analysis, discourse analysis and introspection are techniques which require verbal data. Verbal protocol analysis and protocol analysis are, for the purposes of this book, interchangeable terms. Discourse analysis describes a very different methodology, although one which still uses verbal data. Introspection is a different methodology again, although it is the one most frequently confused with verbal protocol analysis. The distinctions between all these different methodologies are clarified in Chapter 1.

Verbal reports and verbal data may sometimes both be used to refer to the data which are gathered using protocol analysis. However, verbal data is in practice the more generalisable term in that data gathered using other techniques, such as discourse analysis or interviewing, may also be described as verbal data. The term verbal report is used throughout this book to refer specifically to data gathered using protocol analysis. The term verbal data is used to refer to data gathered using other techniques.

The book is written as a guide to the technique of verbal protocol analysis with a view to demonstrating to the practitioner in language testing how to apply the technique across a range of situations. With this aim in mind, a number of example scenarios are described within each section. Different aspects of the same two studies are used as worked examples across the chapters to illustrate different approaches and to provide the reader with a detailed breakdown of all the issues under consideration at different stages. Tutorial exercises are presented so that the reader can try out the technique before applying it in real life contexts.

The chapters take the reader through the methodology in a systematic fashion. Chapter 1 first outlines the technique and then describes each of the steps involved in using verbal protocol analysis. The theoretical background to protocol analysis is presented and evaluated. The validity and reliability of the technique are discussed here, and some of the major applications for verbal protocol analysis are described. Verbal reports are not all produced in the same manner. Chapter 1 describes some of the main distinctions: think aloud versus talk aloud, concurrent versus retrospective, and mediated versus non-mediated verbalisation. Finally, the chapter considers different validation questions for language testing that may be addressed using verbal protocol analysis.

Chapter 2 focuses on data preparation and collection. This chapter describes the decisions and processes involved in selecting an appropriate task and gathering verbal reports. The role of a task analysis is described and the procedure for carrying out a task analysis is presented. A question to consider in using verbal protocol analysis is whether to collect supplementary data. This issue is addressed in Chapter 2, with examples of situations where supplementary data may be useful, and guidelines on the kind of supplemen-

Preface

tary data that may be collected. Detailed instructions to help elicit verbal protocols are presented, with extracts from verbal protocols to illustrate each procedure. Issues to consider in transcribing data are discussed. Two worked examples are presented to illustrate the processes described in Chapter 2. The tutorial exercise at the end of the chapter provides practice in using these techniques.

Chapter 3 discusses in detail the steps involved in developing a coding scheme for verbal protocols. The issues to be considered include the identification of what will comprise a unit for analysis, how to segment a protocol and how to develop the coding scheme that will be used to code the protocol. Examples illustrating some different approaches to these steps are presented within each section, with two fully worked examples to illustrate the entire phase of developing a coding scheme. A tutorial exercise at the end of the chapter provides the reader with an example upon which to base the development of a coding scheme.

Chapter 4 moves on to describe the actual coding and analysis of verbal protocol data. Some of the issues to be discussed here include establishing the reliability of codings and different ways to carry out the coding of data. The chapter looks at some different techniques for analysing data, using examples to illustrate each approach. Some guidance on appropriate statistical techniques is provided. The worked examples show how some of these techniques were used in analysing verbal protocol data. Finally, the tutorial exercise presents the reader with opportunities for trying out some of the techniques.

Chapter 5 provides an overview of the main themes and issues presented in the book. In particular, Chapter 5 considers the multidimensionality of skills, and examines the implications of this for approaches to construct validation.

1 Verbal protocol analysis

Introduction

This chapter describes the methodology of verbal protocol analysis and considers the range of validation questions that might be addressed using this methodology in the domain of language testing. Specifically, we consider:

- What is verbal protocol analysis?
- The different categories of verbal protocols
- The theoretical background
- Validity and reliability of verbal reports
- Some applications for verbal protocol analysis
- The procedure for carrying out verbal protocol analysis
- What are the disadvantages in using verbal protocols?
- A range of validation questions

What is verbal protocol analysis?

Verbal protocol analysis (VPA) distinguishes itself from other techniques that employ verbal data because, in the case of VPA, inferences are actually made about the cognitive processes that produced the verbalisation. In this way, it differs from other techniques, such as discourse analysis or interviewing, which focus primarily on linguistic content and structure, and the formation of what is said.

'Verbal protocol' is a special label used to describe the data gathered from an individual under special conditions, where the person is asked to either 'talk aloud' or to 'think aloud'. The 'protocol' comprises the utterances made by the individual. The protocol might contain the utterances made as the individual carries out a single task, or a series of tasks. A set of protocols might be gathered from different individuals completing similar tasks, or from the same individual completing different tasks. The set of protocols gathered constitute a body of qualitative data.

Verbal protocol analysis is a methodology which is based on the assertion that an individual's verbalisations may be seen to be an accurate record of

1 Verbal protocol analysis

information that is (or has been) attended to as a particular task is (or has been) carried out. Usually, the individual is asked either to think aloud or 'talk aloud'[1] as the task is carried out. Sometimes the individual is asked to verbalise retrospectively, after the task has been carried out.

Protocol analysis is considered to be a qualitative methodology in that standard statistical procedures cannot be directly applied to the verbal report data. Inferences may be made directly from the data without the need to quantify the data for numerical analyses. For instance, some studies aim to examine the content and sequence of information that is contained within the verbal protocol, while others might focus on the content alone.

Some studies seek to quantify the data in particular ways, perhaps looking at the frequency with which certain behaviours occur. In such cases, the data need to be transformed through coding of individual segments prior to analysis. Various statistical analyses may then be carried out, perhaps to compare the protocols of different groups of subjects, or to construct profiles of cognitive activity as different tasks are carried out by different individuals. The data that comprise the verbal protocols then may, if the study requires it, be subjected to both qualitative and quantitative analyses.

The methodology lends itself to a wide range of applications in cognitive psychology, educational psychology, psychology of assessment, cognitive science, and social psychology. It has been used to investigate cognitive processes involved in learning a programming language (Anderson, Farrell and Sauers 1984), to identify processes involved in text comprehension (Laszlo, Meutsch and Viehoff 1988), to examine interactions between different categories of behaviour in mathematical problem solving (Schoenfeld 1983), to help specify the mental representations used by expert and novice mathematical problem solvers (Schoenfeld and Herrmann 1982), and to explore differences between experts and novices solving political science problems (Voss, Greene, Post and Penner 1983). The technique has also been used by both Green and Gilhooly (1990 a and b) and Thorndyke and Stasz (1980) in studies seeking to identify cognitive processes differentiating good from poorer learners. These studies sought to facilitate learning by instructing novices in the use of the learning strategies and procedures found to be used by efficient learners.

Verbal protocol analysis is currently also used as a means for supplementing data obtained from quantitative techniques in the field of testing and assessment, where the validity of the instrument and the reliability of judgements are key concerns. Many of the more traditional, quantitative ap-proaches have tended to focus on the issue of reliability. Reliability con-

1 The distinction between 'think aloud' and the rather similar 'talk aloud' is elaborated later in this chapter. For now, we may note that the think aloud procedure produces similar information to the talk aloud, plus some information that would not ordinarily be verbalised under talk aloud conditions.

cerns the extent to which we can be sure that judgements of ability or performance are consistent and free from error. Verbal protocol analysis can be used with more conventional quantitative approaches, such as item analysis, to examine different sources of error. For instance, between-rater error may be high if raters cannot agree on their assessment of a particular individual's ability. Verbal protocols may be gathered from these raters as they carry out the task in order to collect information on the sources of disagreement. The verbal protocols may show evidence of erroneous reasoning by raters, failure to note relevant features in a student's work that should be credited, or the use of criteria other than those recommended. Any one of these factors would reduce consistency of ratings. Importantly, this sort of information may not be directly inferred through the application of standard, quantitative approaches.

Verbal protocols are increasingly playing a vital role in the validation of assessment instruments and methods. For instance, Norris (1991) used verbal protocol analysis as part of the process for validating the use of multiple choice questions. Validation investigates whether a test measures the ability or skill that it claims to measure. However, 'validity' is not an attribute that may be established by addressing a single validity question, but rather requires a number of questions to be addressed. One of the aims of this book is to describe a range of validity questions in the field of language testing that might be addressed using protocol analysis.

Verbal protocols offer a means for more directly gathering evidence that supports judgements regarding validity than some of the other more quantitative methods. For example, one of the most fundamental questions centres on establishing what a test actually measures. The test developer will have constructed the test with a particular skill or set of skills in mind. A question to address might be: How accurate has the test developer's characterisation of the skill been? One approach to addressing this question is to ask students to think aloud as they work through a series of test items. The resulting protocols are then analysed in order to identify the cognitive processes involved in carrying out the task. Simply put, if there is a close match between the processes that are actually used, and those the test developer predicts will be used, then the test may be said to measure what it purports to measure. Of course, this is a simplification and ignores a range of other important questions, which we shall encounter later.

The issue of validation may become complex when what a test measures varies from individual to individual, and across time. Research on the acquisition and performance of cognitive skills (see Green and Gilhooly 1992 for a review of this area) shows that as skill develops, knowledge is acquired and this knowledge becomes increasingly organised around domain-relevant principles. There are therefore both quantitative and qualitative differences in knowledge possessed by experts and novices, both between and within these two groups. As skill develops, different strategies evolve in order to carry out

1 Verbal protocol analysis

tasks more efficiently within the domain in question. These strategies tend to be domain-specific in that they do not transfer across domains. For example, a chess expert is unlikely to show superior performance in the domain of physics. There are also differences within groups of individuals who may be classified as novices, or as intermediates, or as experts. Verbal protocol analysis has been extensively used to examine changes in knowledge and process as skill develops, and the findings from this research have important implications, both for our understanding of construct validation, and for approaches to validation. We return to these issues later in this chapter and also in subsequent chapters.

A particularly important point to make is that the methodology of verbal protocol analysis differs in kind from that used many years ago by the early introspectionists. Introspectionism assumes that the individual can directly report the mental processing that gives rise to different sensations and experiences. Verbal protocol theory makes no such claims. We know that individuals cannot directly report their own cognitive processes. The verbal protocol serves as a source of data for the researcher to infer cognitive processes and attended information. Whilst it could be said that protocol analysis evolved from introspection, it differs from introspection in a number of ways. Most important is that protocol analysis requires subjects to express their thoughts, but not to infer the processes that produced those thoughts. Mental processes are inferred afterwards by the researcher.

Cognitive processes then may be inferred from verbal reports but not directly reported by individuals producing such a report. We elaborate on this point later in this chapter. Next we consider in detail the nature of the data that may be gathered using the methodology of verbal protocol analysis.

The different categories of verbal protocols

Verbal protocol analysis is widely used as a means for inferring thought processes and attended information from behaviour. The terms 'verbal report' or 'verbal protocol' will be used specifically to refer to verbalisation which has been generated by an individual following instructions to either talk aloud or think aloud. Under these special conditions, the subject is asked either to tell the researcher all that s/he is thinking as the task is being carried out, or to provide this information retrospectively after the task has been completed. Sometimes the individual is asked questions, and these questions may vary in generality. The instructions that may be used to encourage individuals to produce any of these types of verbal report are described later in this chapter. Some sample instructions are presented in Chapter 2, where we discuss data collection procedures.

Verbal protocols may be gathered in slightly different ways and under varying circumstances, depending on the type of research question that is to

1 Verbal protocol analysis

be addressed. When deciding on an appropriate approach to employ, it may be useful to work with Figure 1 below.

In our selection of approach, we must first determine whether the report is to be a 'talk aloud' or a 'think aloud' report. Next, we should consider when the report is to be produced. We label this the 'temporal' dimension. Individuals may be prompted in different ways as the report is produced. Prompting, or 'mediation', ranges from fairly non-invasive requests, such as 'Tell me what you are thinking at the moment', to more directed prompts such as, 'Could you explain why you did that?' Verbal reports then may be classified as 'mediated' or 'non-mediated'. This may be considered a 'procedural' variation. The main characteristics of each of these variants are described later in this chapter.

Figure 1:

Some variations on the verbal report procedure

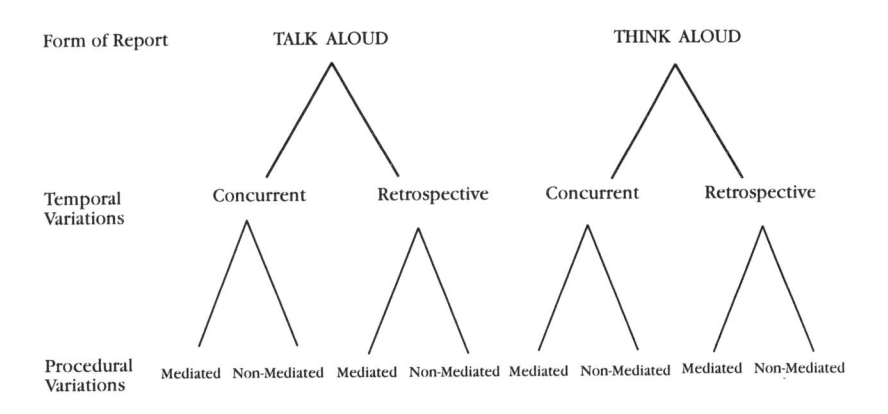

Form of Report: TALK ALOUD, THINK ALOUD

Temporal Variations: Concurrent, Retrospective, Concurrent, Retrospective

Procedural Variations: Mediated, Non-Mediated, Mediated, Non-Mediated, Mediated, Non-Mediated, Mediated, Non-Mediated

First we examine the different verbal reports and variations on the procedure. Whatever the circumstances, the report produced will normally be spoken and tape recorded. The recordings are then transcribed and the data contained therein form the basis for the analysis.

Form of report

In talk aloud, the report produced will include information that is already encoded in verbal form. Put simply, the information contained in these sorts of reports roughly corresponds to words in the mind, or thoughts that might be spoken.

In think aloud, the report produced includes information already encoded in verbal form, as above, plus information that may not originally have been

1 Verbal protocol analysis

encoded in verbal form. This non-verbal information must be transformed and then verbalised. An example of the kind of non-verbal information referred to here might be information about the spatial location of some item or piece of text. Think aloud then has advantages over talk aloud for tasks where individuals may attend to non-verbal information.

The theoretical distinction between talk aloud and think aloud is discussed and illustrated in the Theorical background section below.

Temporal variations

Concurrent (simultaneous) reports are generated at the same time as the individual is working on the task. A person working under these conditions will then produce either a talk aloud or a think aloud report while s/he carries out the task.

Retrospective (subsequent) reports are generated after the individual has finished working on the task. Typically, the person will carry out the task, and will then be asked to verbalise once the task is complete. The time interval between task completion and start of the verbal report is important. If the retrospective report is produced immediately upon completion of the task, much information will still be present in working memory. If there is some delay between task completion and production of the verbal report, then the retrieval process must be considered, and retrieval is of course fallible. Compounding this problem is that of the possible filtering or 'tidying up' of information for a retrospective report. Some individuals may report what they believe the researcher requires, omitting information that was heeded at the time the task was carried out, or may adapt the report in other ways to give the impression of completeness or coherence.

Concurrent reports are far less susceptible to influences from unwanted variables than are retrospective reports. This is a principal factor in favour of the use of concurrent reports wherever possible. For some tasks however, retrospective reports may be the only viable option. We return to these issues later.

Procedural variations

In 'Non-mediated verbalisations', the individual is asked to think aloud and is prompted only when s/he pauses for a period of time. The prompts tend to be as non-intrusive as possible, and would include requests to 'keep talking' for instance. Non-mediated verbalisation may be used to gather either concurrent or retrospective reports.

In 'Mediated verbalisations', the individual may be asked questions about the task, e.g. 'Why did you do that?', and 'What were you referring to just then?' The probing may take place as the task is being carried out or afterwards.

These sorts of verbalisation procedures involve mediating processes before verbalisation, like requests for explanations, justifications, and so on. The relation between heeded states and the verbal report for this procedure is discussed and illustrated in the section below.

Regardless of the procedure used, the same basic assumption underlies the methodology of protocol analysis. We describe the theoretical background in the next section.

Theoretical background

The fundamental underlying assumption for protocol analysis is that information that is heeded as a task is being carried out is represented in a limited capacity short-term memory, and may be reported following an instruction to either talk aloud or think aloud. Ericsson and Simon (1993) state the following: 'We proposed that cognitive processes could be described as sequences of heeded information and cognitive structures, and that verbal reports corresponded to this heeded information'. This is essentially the only assumption made by the theoretical framework described by Ericsson and Simon. No assumptions or claims are made about the nature of the short-term store, or about the nature of the mental representations that embody the attended information. The framework itself does not make any commitments towards a particular model of cognition. The methodology of verbal protocol analysis, then, is best seen as a tool the researcher may use to test hypotheses.

First we elaborate on the distinction between two procedures which were introduced earlier, talk aloud and think aloud. The states of heeded information in a cognitive process are shown below in Figures 2(a) and 2(b), modified from Ericsson and Simon (1993). Figure 2(a) illustrates the relationship between verbalised information and cognitive states under 'talk aloud' conditions. Figure 2(b) illustrates the relationship between verbalised information and cognitive states under 'think aloud' conditions.

The distinction between talk aloud and think aloud is quite subtle, but it is important. Under talk aloud instructions, all that is verbalised is information that is already encoded in verbal form. An important point though is that in carrying out a task, individuals are likely to attend to more than just verbal information. They may also encode non-verbal visual or auditory information, or tactile information. The think aloud procedure then makes it clear that what is verbalised is all heeded information. Thus, information that is not already in verbalisable form (e.g. visual information) may have to be recoded prior to verbalisation. This distinction underlines the requirement that instructions to individuals are precise, stressing that either a think aloud or a talk aloud protocol is required. Given that thinking aloud differs from talking aloud, it is important that the researcher understands which procedure best suits the task at hand. We should note at this point that there is some debate about the

1 Verbal protocol analysis

utility of the distinction between talk aloud and think aloud. In principle, such a distinction appears logical and justifiable. In practice, however, the distinction can be more difficult to maintain. Ericsson and Simon (1993) note that individuals asked to generate verbal reports cannot always distinguish the two. We propose then that the think aloud procedure be adopted for any task that may require subjects to attend to non-verbal information.

Figures 2(a) and 2(b):
The relation between heeded and verbalised information for the talk aloud and think aloud procedures

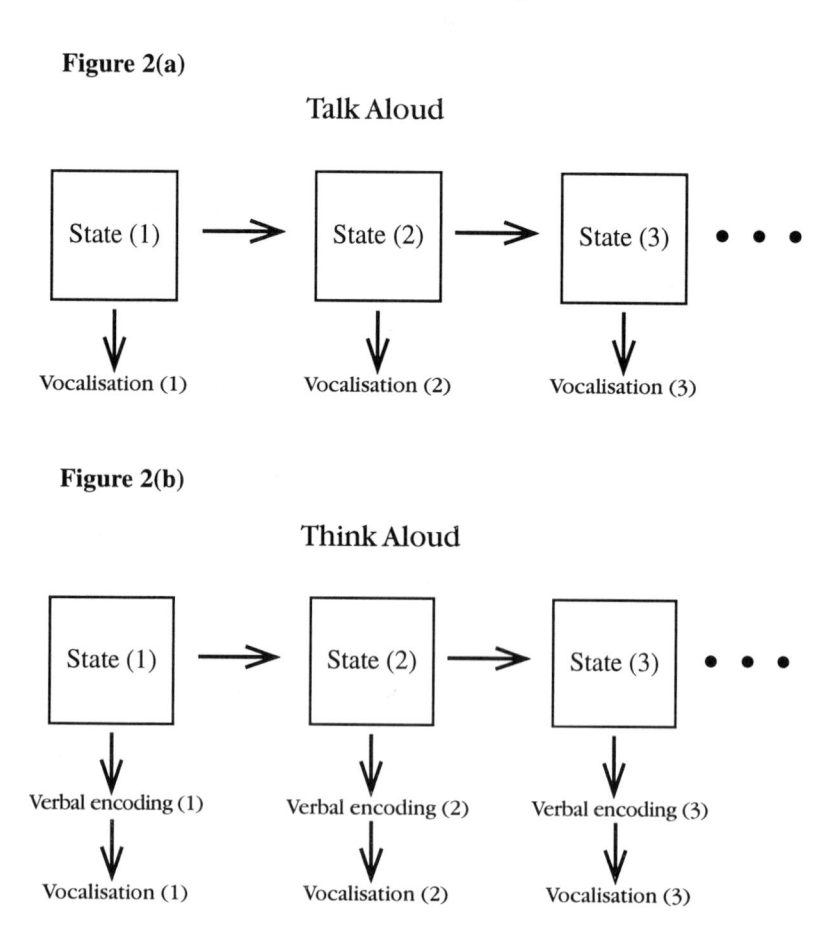

Figure 2(a)

Talk Aloud

State (1) → State (2) → State (3) • • •
   ↓   ↓   ↓
Vocalisation (1) Vocalisation (2) Vocalisation (3)

Figure 2(b)

Think Aloud

State (1) → State (2) → State (3) • • •
   ↓   ↓   ↓
Verbal encoding (1) Verbal encoding (2) Verbal encoding (3)
   ↓   ↓   ↓
Vocalisation (1) Vocalisation (2) Vocalisation (3)

Neither talk aloud nor think aloud should change the structure of the process that is actively engaged in carrying out the main task. Recoding information into a format that enables it to be verbalised may take time, and so an

1 Verbal protocol analysis

individual thinking aloud might take longer to complete the task than an individual who is not generating any verbal report.

A third category of verbalisation requires the individual to explain and interpret certain thoughts. This is termed 'mediation'. Figure 3 illustrates the relationship between verbalised information and cognitive states for mediated procedures.

Figure 3:
The relation between the heeded and verbalised information for mediated procedures

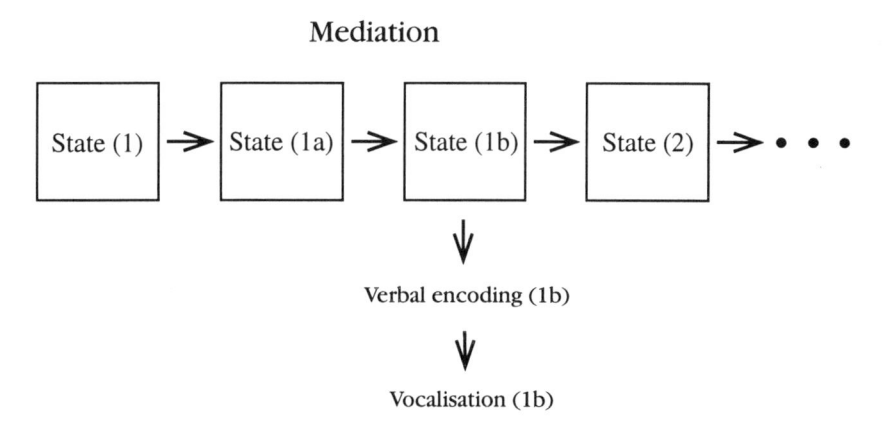

Mediation

State (1) → State (1a) → State (1b) → State (2) → • • •

↓

Verbal encoding (1b)

↓

Vocalisation (1b)

A difficulty with verbal reports produced under mediating conditions is that the natural sequence of behaviour can be altered. Questions that are geared to probe for information at particular points as the protocol is produced can force individuals to switch their attention to what is being requested of them and to process information that might not otherwise have been processed. Ballstaedt and Mandl (1984) found that recall of a text was improved for those individuals asked to elaborate the text aloud, compared with a control group who read silently. This sort of interference by specific instructions, which can culminate in improved learning or recall performance, may have useful pedagogical applications.

Some tasks may be more resistant to interference from probes. Norris (1991) compared the performance of five different groups of subjects taking a critical thinking test. One group produced concurrent verbal reports while three other groups produced immediate reports under probe conditions. A fifth group worked under normal test conditions, without any requirements to verbalise. In this case, there were no differences in performance between the groups, and more surprisingly, no evidence of differences in reported information between the groups. Probes, if used, must be carefully worded to reduce the likelihood of intermediate and inferential processing, both of which could change the natural sequence of heeded information.

Talk aloud and think aloud reports may be gathered concurrently or retrospectively, or both. There are potential difficulties with retrospective reports though. The principal problem is that a retrospective account involves an additional process, recovering information from memory. Whether or not there is a delay between task completion and production of the verbal report, retrospective reports may be subject to two further problems. The first of these is that heeded information may be omitted in the report, and redundant information might be included. The second problem is that it can be difficult to separate information attended to as the task was carried out from information acquired or attended to after (or even before) the task was completed. The report may be contaminated by a subject's efforts to 'tidy up' what happened, or to rationalise what occurred. Concurrent verbalisations closely match the flow of attention to information as the task is being carried out and so are far less likely to be susceptible to these problems. It is therefore best to collect concurrent verbal reports, unless the task dictates otherwise.

Validity and reliability of verbal reports

Validity and reliability are two closely related concerns. In the context of verbal protocol analysis, we need to distinguish between validity and reliability of the technique, and validity and reliability of the coded data. In educational assessment, validity and reliability have quite particular meanings. For instance, as educationists, we distinguish between different aspects of validity, and between different factors that serve to reduce reliability. In psychological research, concerns about the validity and reliability of a technique, or data, are both expressed and addressed in slightly different ways.

We begin by considering the validity and reliability of the technique and then go on to consider validity and reliability of encodings of verbal protocol data.

Validity of the technique

In this context, 'validity' centres on whether information that is captured within verbal reports corresponds with information that is actually heeded as a task is carried out. If verbal reports were shown to be incomplete, or if information within them were susceptible to distortion, or if verbal reports included additional information that may not have been heeded as the task was carried out, then the validity of the technique might be questioned.

Thus, the validity of verbal reports depends crucially upon the extent to which information that is actually heeded as a task is being carried out corresponds closely with what is then verbalised, and the extent to which the task may be carried out without disruption by the requirement to generate a verbal report. Ericsson and Simon (1993) review a very large number of studies which indicate that, when the technique is used appropriately, verbal protocol analysis is a valid and useful procedure. Of course, it is impossible to prove that verbalised information actually reflects information that is heeded as a task is carried out. It is however possible to show that there are close correspondences between what is verbalised and the behaviour of the individual. For instance, that certain information is heeded may be supported by examining videotapes made as the task was carried out.

Validity is maximised by adhering to certain principles in the procedure. First, it is important to ensure that appropriate instructions are used in order to guide the production of the verbal report. Individuals must be discouraged from trying to explain or rationalise their thoughts. The verbal report should ideally be produced as the task is being carried out, with minimum intervention from the researcher. A delay between completing the task and producing the verbal report can introduce 'error' – information may be lost from memory, additional information heeded after the task has been completed may be incorporated into the representation of what took place, or the original account of what took place may be altered in some respect as a result of cognitive processing occurring after the event. Most of these problems may be avoided by using the concurrent procedure.

The reader is referred to Ericsson and Simon (1993) for a fuller discussion of the validity of the technique, and specifically to their evaluation of the criticisms of Nisbett and Wilson (1977). Briefly stated, Nisbett and Wilson's criti-cisms of the technique stem largely from studies which indicate that individuals cannot always report reliably on relevant information which appears to have influenced their particular judgements or decisions. There are two principal difficulties with the Nisbett and Wilson criticisms. The first is that the verbal report procedures they describe were inadequate, introducing time lags during which valuable information could be lost. The second is that subjects appear to have been asked about their cognitive processes. Given that it is not possible to report directly on cognitive processes, it is not surprising that subjects speculated about why they behaved as they did.

Reliability of the technique

In this context, reliability of the technique refers principally to the likelihood that similar verbal reports might be produced by the same individual presented with the same or very similar tasks. The existence of individual differences means that we cannot assume that different people presented with the same or similar tasks will behave in very similar ways. Reliability of the technique is of course dependent upon the extent to which the coding scheme accurately captures behaviour and so reliability of the technique is related to validity of the coding scheme. An inadequate coding scheme will most certainly bias the researcher towards incorrect inferences about behaviour.

If an individual were to produce very different reports in response to the same task and under identical circumstances, then we might question not just the reliability of the technique, but also its validity. Fortunately, there is a good deal of evidence to support the proposition that individuals are consistent. For instance, research in the domains of mathematics (Schoenfeld and Herrmann 1980) and physics (Chi, Glaser and Rees 1982) suggests that intra-individual differences are considerably less marked than are inter-individual differences. Individuals varying in skill level produce quite different verbal protocols, as one might expect, but individuals at similar skill levels produce verbal protocols that share at least some important similarities.

Reliability of reports is complicated by individual differences, and by the effects of contextual and task variables. Not all individuals approach tasks in the same way, and so different strategies are often in evidence. Context exercises a considerable influence on the probability that information available for use in one situation may be recoverable for use in another situation. Task variables also exert an influence. Structuring similar tasks in different ways may call for different cognitive processes, and may influence both what is heeded and the way in which this is achieved. However, task variables and individual differences influence performance in fairly systematic ways. Individuals are sufficiently consistent to allow us to conclude that verbal protocol analysis is reliable. Differences within groups of individuals are more likely to be attributable to task, situational or individual difference variables than to lack of reliability of the technique.

Validity of the encoded data

The validity of codings addresses the issue of whether or not a code for a given protocol accurately captures cognitive processes and heeded information as the task was carried out. This may be indirectly assessed by, for instance, comparing the pattern of behaviour indicated by the verbal protocol with some supporting information. This could be a record of key presses made while a computing task was carried out, or a videotape of eye fixations as a perceptual task was carried out. Validity of codings is related to reliability of codings, which is discussed below. If two coders were asked to develop a coding scheme independently and to analyse the verbal reports using their respective coding schemes, one would hope that similar categories would emerge and that segments of protocol would be coded using these similar categories.

Reliability of the encoded data

The issue of reliability of encoded data centres on the probability that the same data might be coded using the same categories, either by two independent encoders, or by the same individual coding the set of protocols twice.

Reliability of codings of verbal reports is usually assessed by ensuring that at least two individuals code either the full set of reports, or a proportion of the full set. The proportion of instances where agreement is reached is measured and the overall reliability estimate is this proportion. High agreement is a good indicator of inter-coder reliability.

Reliability of encoded data may be reduced, however, by transcriber and encoder variables. The transcriber's task is to convert the spoken words into visual form, without altering the transcript in any way. This can require some skill in order to disambiguate certain utterances. It also requires the transcriber to encode pauses and silences which may be of importance.

Encoders are unlikely to be asked both to segment and encode the verbal protocols. Instead, the encoders are more likely to be asked to encode protocols once segmentation has been carried out. In assessing reliability, it is important to ensure that both encoders are sufficiently skilled and familiar with the task to offset any unwanted influence of encoder variables.

Summary

Verbal reports are now widely used, and provided that the researcher adheres to certain rules in using protocol analysis, the methodology can be valid, reliable and useful. In the next section, the range of different applications for the technique is presented.

Some applications for verbal protocol analysis

Verbal protocols are used extensively by researchers working in the areas of cognitive modelling, expert systems development, investigations of cognitive processes involved in learning and performing a range of different skills, as well as in the area of assessment. Figure 4 describes the procedure for gathering information from an expert in order to incorporate this into an expert system. The knowledge engineer acquires the relevant domain knowledge from the domain expert, and this is then built into the expert system. Much the same sort of procedure is adopted in the field of language assessment. The test developer may produce a specification of a given language at a particular level of proficiency. This then guides the development of an assessment geared towards assessing language skill at the level in question.

There are a range of assessment questions that may be addressed using protocol analysis. The principal questions centre on issues of validity – for instance, does the assessment instrument accurately measure the skills or abilities it aims to measure?

An important point to note is that, for most applications, the language used by the individual generating the verbal report is not in itself the focal point for the research. The content of the verbal report is of course critical, but the precise

1 Verbal protocol analysis

wording is a secondary concern. This is because, for most applications, the language used is simply a vehicle for expressing what information is currently being heeded. Coding schemes typically categorise an utterance as an instance of a particular class of verbalisation.

Figure 4:
Typical knowledge acquisition process for building an expert system

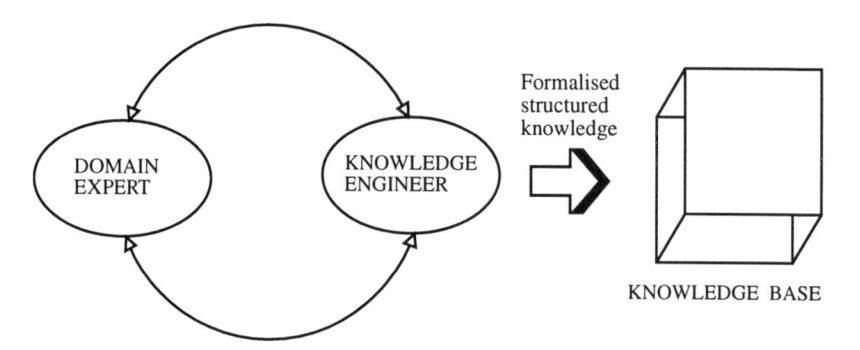

However, in the case of language research, what counts is not just what is verbalised but also how this is achieved. Thus, the focus becomes the content of the verbalisation (such as extent of vocabulary, grammatical accuracy and so on) and the manner of verbalisation (such as fluency).

The next section examines the procedure for gathering and analysing verbal reports. Each of these steps is elaborated and discussed at length in subsequent chapters.

The procedure for carrying out VPA

The first and most important question to consider is whether or not the particular application in mind is one for which protocol analysis is suited. There are numerous examples of instances where a particular technique is applied because it is fashionable to do so. The limitations of any technique must be recognised. Protocol analysis does not lend itself to all applications. Like most other methodologies, it is best used to address a particular class of research question. In the context of language testing, these are predominantly questions centring on the validation process. Some questions that might be asked are:

- Does the test in question actually measure the set of skills it purports to measure?

1 Verbal protocol analysis

- Do two different versions of the same test measure the same skills?
- To what extent do two or more different tests that are assumed to measure the same skills actually measure the same skills?
- Does a particular item type, such as multiple choice, require the same skills as another item type, such as an open-ended or free response format?
- Are some item types more effective measures of the skill in question than others?
- Does the content of a particular item influence performance?
- Do raters heed the marking criteria in assessing performance on the task in question?
- Do rater variables influence judgements in undesirable ways?

Regardless of the task or domain, there are a series of distinct phases in gathering and analysing verbal reports. These are:

- Task identification
- Task analysis
- Selecting an appropriate procedure
- Selecting subjects
- Training subjects
- Collecting verbal reports
- Collecting supplementary data
- Transcribing verbal reports
- Developing an encoding scheme
- Segmenting protocols
- Encoding protocols
- Calculating encoder reliability
- Analysing data

We shall briefly describe each phase in turn. The phases are discussed in considerable detail in Chapters 2, 3 and 4.

1 Verbal protocol analysis

Task identification

The first phase involves identifying a suitable task, although this label is a misnomer to some extent since it is often the case that the 'task' is defined and it is a methodology that requires identification. Nevertheless, identification is a particularly important step in the process as it defines a priori the range of acceptable models that could generate the desired behaviour or response. Identifying an appropriate task is not always straightforward, though, as we shall see in Chapter 2.

Task analysis

Pre-determined procedures and coding schemes, for analysing protocols gathered as different tasks are carried out, do not exist. Thus, the researcher must set about developing an understanding of what is entailed in carrying out the task in question. For instance, when asked to multiply the numbers 25 and 36 together, people are known to use different strategies. The task analysis should, to a certain extent, enable the researcher to consider some of the possible ways in which the task in question might be carried out. The task ana-lysis then forms the basis for the coding scheme. An additional function of the task analysis is to develop ways to formalise some of the terminology that is specific to the task. For example, if the task requires the person to read from four different pieces of text, then the task analysis will identify each piece and allocate a label to each. A task analysis also provides a means for aggregating information under like categories.

Selecting an appropriate procedure

Next, the researcher must decide which procedure to use: talk aloud or think aloud, concurrent or retrospective, mediated or unmediated. The differences between each were discussed earlier. Concurrent reports are generally preferred to retrospective reports.

Selecting subjects

In the domain of language testing, protocols are most likely to be gathered from subjects who are representative of the group who might take the test in question, and from raters or examiners who might actually assess performance on the test in question.

Training subjects

Subjects generally need to be trained before being used in any study. This will involve a familiarisation with the technique itself and the reasons for conducting the study. In addition, it is very useful for them to practise and be

1 Verbal protocol analysis

given feedback from the researcher before starting. Without this sort of training and familiarisation, data are likely to be heavily flawed.

Collecting verbal reports

Before any analysis can begin, the verbal reports must be gathered, either by tape or on video. These are the most reliable means for gathering complete information. Note-taking or selective data gathering techniques are not suitable methods for gathering data for protocol analysis simply because the resulting data are not a complete transcript. Inferences may only reliably be made from verbal reports when those data are complete and unaltered. Thus, a structured interview with a candidate or examiner may provide interesting data, but these data would not constitute a verbal report and could not be treated as such.

Collecting supplementary data

Supplementary information may be gathered, although this step should be considered optional. For instance, the researcher may wish to interview the candidate after the verbal report has been gathered in order to test aspects of memory, or to gather information on strategies candidates may have used to carry out the task. Sometimes additional data may be recorded too, e.g. a record of key presses, if the task is one involving computer use. Additional data can be particularly useful if it is not clear from a subject's report what information is being attended to, or indeed whether any task-relevant information is currently the focus of attention. Information in 'focal attention' may be assumed to be information that is currently active and subject to cognitive processing. We may also be consciously aware of information that is in focal attention. Supplementary data may be used to clarify what is going on, but should not replace the verbal report.

Transcribing verbal reports

Once gathered, the verbal reports are transcribed. Frequently this requires an audio-typist to listen to the tape and to transcribe it in its entirety. It is recommended that researchers adopt a system where time markers are used. For instance, a marker might be used after each ten seconds of verbalisation, and to indicate the duration of pauses. This can give an indication of how much time is spent on a particular aspect of a task for instance, or how much time is spent within a particular phase of cognitive activity. Such markers may also be used to infer when difficulties or 'impasses' are met – individuals often fall silent when encountering task difficulties. Time markers allow inferences to be made about how time was apportioned, and this can be extremely valuable in comparing groups of individuals.

1 Verbal protocol analysis

Developing an encoding scheme

Verbal protocols are usually transformed in order to facilitate analysis. The principal way in which this is achieved is by developing a scheme for coding segments of protocol. Different people verbalise things in different ways. Similarities between two statements may only appear when those statements are considered at deeper levels. Thus, two superficially different statements might have more in common than at first appears. This is essentially the purpose of an encoding scheme – to develop coding categories that capture commonalities between behaviours in order that a range of common classes of behaviour may be identified for a given task or situation.

The development of an encoding scheme is necessarily shaped by the aims of the study, and by the task analysis. We discuss these issues in depth in Chapter 3.

Broad aims might include:

- the construction of computer models to model processes, e.g. in reading
- the testing of hypotheses, e.g. investigating whether or not a particular strategy is used to rate an essay
- developing a general characterisation of the skill in question, e.g. translating text from French to English
- at a more specific level, the aims of the study might be to understand the development of strategies used for a particular task, such as translation

The task analysis will suggest a range of possible strategies that might be used in order to carry out the task. If we consider the task of translation, translators of different skill might approach a task in quite different ways, translating different units of text. A task analysis should identify the likely units for our translation example. Similarly, if we take the example of reading, the task analysis should identify different sections of text that might be read in order to answer a particular question, and might also specify ways in which text might be read – simple reading, reading with paraphrasing and reading with interpretation are some examples of different approaches to reading.

A random sample of perhaps ten per cent of the protocols may be used to first develop the coding categories. In constructing a coding scheme for the analysis of verbal reports, a theoretical framework may be used to guide the analysis of data. The researcher may develop a framework based on a particular theory. This theory may make weak predictions, focusing on information that is heeded, or may make stronger predictions about the sequences of processes associated with accurate performance. Whichever approach is

1 Verbal protocol analysis

adopted, one important point made by Ericsson and Simon (1993) is that the framework for analysing protocols should allow for the testing of hypotheses that are consistent with the selected theory and those that might be predicted by other theories.

Segmenting protocols

Protocols are segmented, each segment corresponding to a chunk of behaviour, such as a statement or a phrase. These segments would then comprise the units for analysis. An alternative approach is to identify much larger segments, corresponding to several sentences, with a single event or task as the focus. These more macroscopic analyses may focus on broad episodes of behaviour where an episode itself would constitute the unit for analysis. Some of the more microscopic approaches tend to focus on much smaller sequences of behaviour. The key issue is to determine what is to represent a unit for analysis – a clause, phrase, sentence or group of sentences.

Encoding protocols

Each segment of a protocol should be unambiguously assigned one code. If the coding scheme has been developed following good procedure, then ambiguity should be minimised. However, it is always the case that some segments of protocol present the encoder with difficulties. The segment may be very brief, or it may appear that one sentence is begun and verbalisation ceases before the sentence is complete. These sorts of segments can be problematic. Segments that cannot be unambiguously encoded should be assigned a special code. We discuss in Chapter 4 ways to deal with ambiguity.

Calculating encoder reliability

After the encoding stage, protocols should be encoded by at least two coders. Inter-coder reliability is computed by assessing the extent to which two coders agree on the codes assigned to each segment within a protocol. It is necessary to show that inter-coder agreement is better than chance. Inter-coder reliability is influenced by the extent to which coders must make inferences, and the extent to which coding of segments is carried out independently of other segments. High agreement (80 per cent and above) is usually sought between coders. More fine-grained schemes may have the negative consequence of reducing reliability. Even if inter-coder reliability is high, problems may remain. Bias may occur when decisions on how to code are influenced by previous segments, or when coders are knowledgeable about the hypotheses being tested.

Analysing data

Once the protocols have been coded, data are analysed. Coded data may be quantified for submission to analyses such as analysis of variance, or chi-square. Analysis of variance may be used to examine the extent to which two or more groups differ in the frequency with which certain behaviours, cognitive processes or broad strategies are evident in their protocols. Tests of association, such as chi-square or correlation, may be used to examine associations between two or more variables. In this way, protocol analysis can be seen as both a qualitative and a quantitative technique.

Summary

Protocol analysis is a well defined methodology suited to a range of applications. It entails a series of distinct phases which have been described in this section. Each phase is discussed in depth in subsequent chapters.

What are the disadvantages in using verbal protocols?

Whilst verbal protocols are a very rich source of data, there are some drawbacks to the technique, and some pitfalls that may be avoided.

Commitment in time

Arguably the biggest problem in using verbal protocols is that the entire process of gathering and analysing verbal reports tends to be very time consuming. The procedures involved in ensuring that the conditions are appropriate for gathering verbal reports, in transcribing the data, in coding and finally analysing data are very labour intensive. However, the technique does yield a very large amount of rich data.

Disruption of behaviour

There are procedural difficulties in that it can be easy to disrupt and alter behaviour unintentionally. For instance, Ericsson and Simon (1993) note that when subjects fall silent for a period of time, the instruction to 'keep talking' is less disruptive than the instruction, 'Please can you tell me what you are thinking'? The latter is more likely to be interpreted as a direct request for information by the experimenter, whereas the former is more likely to be received as a prompt to continue verbalising. Unless mediation is being used, prompts that might encourage a direct response to the experimenter should be avoided, since these are more likely to disrupt behaviour.

The instructions subjects are given in order to elicit a verbal report should be carefully worded. Some researchers have requested that subjects not only verbalise their thoughts, but also that they try to explain them. These sorts of

1 Verbal protocol analysis

instructions impose additional demands on the subject and consequently alter the way in which the task is approached. If mediation is being used, the researcher must be aware of the ways in which different prompts might alter behaviour.

Individual differences

Coupled with the problem of ensuring that what is recorded is a valid verbal protocol is the issue of individual differences in the production of verbal reports. Gilhooly (1986) found that individuals vary considerably in the quality and quantity of verbal reports produced. He also found that individuals tend to be consistent. Thus, an individual might consistently produce a lengthy report, or might consistently produce a very sparse report. This is an important consideration which tends to be overlooked. If the researcher is to make inferences from verbal reports, then ideally the data produced should be as clean and complete as possible. It is not entirely clear how one should deal with sparse reports, or whether sparse reports are as 'valid' as more extended reports. Some clues may be used to infer whether or not subjects are experiencing any thoughts. Thus, if a subject falls silent but continues with the task, it is probable that relevant thoughts are not being verbalised. These sorts of protocols are likely to provide incomplete records of heeded information as the task was being carried out, and discarding such reports may be the best option.

Summary

We can conclude then that the biggest drawback in using verbal protocol analysis is the amount of time required. Procedural pitfalls can be avoided by paying special attention to instructions used to elicit verbal reports. Data problems can be offset by identifying and discarding incomplete reports.

A range of validation questions

This section considers some different validation questions and how these might be addressed for the different types of language assessment task.

At the beginning of this book, some important considerations were introduced. One was a fairly recent move towards viewing skills as multidimensional, rather than unidimensional. A second consideration is that skills develop over time. Both have important implications for construct validation. Construct validation, as we shall see in the following section, is concerned with gathering evidence to support the validity of interpretations from test scores.

Validity and validation

'Validity' is a complex concept. Although it is has been argued to be a unitary

1 Verbal protocol analysis

concept (Messick 1989), it makes little sense to talk about the 'validity' of a particular test or set of test scores. Validity centres on the extent to which inferences and interpretations from test scores are supported by the evidence available.

In many respects, it makes more sense to talk about the validation process and the different types of validity questions than it does to focus on multiple notions of validity. Bachman (1990) describes validation as 'a general process that consists of the marshaling of evidence to support a given interpretation or use, a process that is based on logical, empirical and ethical considerations' (p. 238).

There are different validity questions then, the importance of each in any one context depending very much on the function of the assessment instrument. Bachman (1990) describes the different types of evidence that might be accumulated as part of the validation process. These map onto the more traditional 'types' of validity described by Cronbach and Meehl (1955) thus:

Bachman taxonomy	**Cronbach and Meehl taxonomy**
Construct validity	Construct validity
Content relevance and content coverage	Content validity
Criterion relatedness	Criterion validity
(i) Predictive utility	(i) Predictive validity
(ii) Concurrent criterion relatedness	(ii) Concurrent validity

Measurement specialists today argue that it is better to view the traditional types of validities as complementary aspects of the unitary concept of validity, than as separable 'types'. Each of the traditional 'types' addresses a different validity question, or a different aspect of the validation process, and thus each allows evidence to be accumulated. Importantly, no one 'type' of evidence could be considered more important than another, and none is sufficient in and of itself to demonstrate the validity of a particular interpretation of test scores, or a particular use of test scores. The validity of interpretations then is clearly limited by the amount of evidence accumulated, and by the nature of that evidence.

We shall now turn to consider each of the different sources of evidence for validity.

'Construct validity' traditionally centred on the extent to which the test items measure a distinct skill or trait. It was differentiated into the subcategories of:

- convergent validity
- discriminant validity

1 Verbal protocol analysis

'Convergent validity' was measured by assessing the degree to which different measures of the same skill or trait correlate. 'Discriminant validity' was concerned with the extent to which a skill or trait is demonstrably distinct from other skills or traits.

A major difference between former and more recent approaches to validity is the elevation of construct validity to a more central and unifying role. Where previously construct validity may have been deemed a distinct 'type' of validity, it is now argued to be the unifying concept that integrates criterion relatedness, and content relevance and content coverage within a single framework. Several types of empirical evidence may be gathered in the process of construct validation. These include:

- correlational data
- experimental data
- analyses of processes underlying test performance (through protocol analysis, computer modelling, errors analysis and so on)

The process of construct validation is now viewed as the process through which all the evidential bases for validity are incorporated. There are difficulties with the view that a construct is the 'something' that is measured by a test. One problem, as alluded to earlier, is that an ability may comprise a series of subskills. A second problem is that the ability in question may develop over time. If the ability in question is multidimensional, and if the subskills making up that ability develop over time, then the 'something' that a test measures may change over time. In effect, the 'construct' may change as the ability develops. Over the initial part of the learning curve, performance on a particular task may largely be a function of subskills a, b and c, whereas later on, performance on the same task may depend more on skills x, y and z. Can we say then that this task measures the same skills in the same way for individuals differing in level of skill development? It appears not, and this is illustrated later when we consider translation skill.

'Content validity' has traditionally been concerned with the degree to which the items or tasks that make up a test accurately and adequately represent the domain in question. The more sophisticated terms of content relevance and content coverage formulate the question rather differently. Content relevance requires that both the ability domain and the facets of test method are specified. Content coverage centres on the tasks selected and whether these adequately represent the domain in question.

'Criterion validity' has traditionally been considered to comprise two 'types': predictive validity and concurrent validity. We now use the superordinate

1 Verbal protocol analysis

term 'criterion relatedness', and the subordinate terms 'predictive utility' and 'concurrent criterion relatedness'.

'Predictive validity' has been described as concerning the degree of correlation between performance on a test and performance on a task that is believed to require the skill or skills that are measured by the test. Predictive utility centres on the same issue, but there is greater awareness now of the dangers inherent in relying on correlational data. Good predictors do not necessarily measure the same abilities. Upshur (1979) discusses some of the problems in using predictive utility in the domain of language testing.

'Concurrent validity' was used to describe the degree of association between different tests that measure the same construct. Concurrent criterion relatedness is used in a similar but more developed fashion. The same problems remain however – can we be sure that the criterion behaviour is an indic-ator of the ability in question? Correlational data cannot be used as evidence for validity unless supported by evidence from construct validation.

Finally, we turn to one other concept which has been discussed in the context of language testing:

- face validity, or test appeal (Bachman 1990)

'Face validity' is about the relationship between the items used to make up a test and the skill in question. Specifically, do the items look as if they measure the skill in question? Face validity has long been a controversial concept in measurement research and practice. The difficulty appears to be that, while there is no theoretical basis for face validity, test appeal is an important consideration in test use.

We turn now to consider the different assessment categories used in language testing and some of the ways in which protocol analysis may be used in construct validation.

Assessment categories

A language test will utilise a range of different assessment categories. The assessment categories represent different skills; thus we might consider an individual's skills in translating, or in reading. The skills may be assessed using different item types. A multiple choice question is an item type, as is an item from a cloze test. For instance, if evidence is required to support the validity of inferences drawn about performance on a multiple choice test, questions will focus on the utility of this class of item type in assessing the skill in question.

The most common assessment categories include:

1 Verbal protocol analysis

- Reading
- Writing
- Translation
- Listening
- Speaking

The same sorts of validation issues arise for each category, but the ways in which these might be addressed using verbal protocol analysis will differ. The validation questions may be elaborated for the categories described above[2] and set in the context of a production and evaluation process for a given assessment instrument. The production process for question papers is discussed in more detail in Chapter 2.

The following sections describe some of the ways that verbal protocol analysis might be used as part of test development and the ongoing evaluation procedures for the different assessment categories.

Reading

Tests of reading, and particularly reading in a foreign language, can be quite well specified, constructed and evaluated. The UCLES First Certificate in English (FCE) Specifications and Sample Papers for the revised FCE examination provides a description of the reading test, specifies the test focus and describes the range of tasks that make up the test. (Paper 1, Reading, is included in Appendix I.)

The UCLES FCE test states that the skills central to reading include understanding:

- gist
- main points
- detail
- text structure or specific information, and
- deducing meaning

Different item types are used to assess skill in reading.

---

2 An exception to this is the oral interview category, which does not lend itself well to protocol analysis. Discourse analysis techniques have been used successfully for this assessment category, for instance, to evaluate raters (Lazaraton 1996).

1 Verbal protocol analysis

One of the ways in which the construct validity of a test such as this may be assessed is by collecting and analysing verbal protocols as candidates complete different tasks. Processes revealed through protocol analysis may be compared with models of the skill in question in order to assess degree of similarity.

If verbal protocol analysis is used to look at the construct validity of multiple choice tests of reading, for example, then a number of issues can be addressed.

At the most basic level, one question centres on whether candidates adapt their behaviour when multiple choice format is used, perhaps guessing, or do they approach the task in much the same way as they would an open-ended reading test. Verbal protocols can provide direct information on cognitive processes and so can address this issue. For instance, verbal protocols might be gathered from students taking the same test either in multiple choice format or in free response format. If both tests measure the same construct, similar processes should be identifiable from the verbal protocols. The processes and sequences of heeded information that are evidenced in the protocols might then be compared with those predicted by a model of reading. It should be possible to differentiate processes related to the task specifically as opposed to the aim of the test. We can elaborate this a bit further.

Freedle and Kostin (1993) describe a study which sought to predict difficulty of TOEFL multiple choice reading items. Their approach was to refer to the background literature on predicting language comprehension item difficulty and to identify those variables that might be expected to influence reading item difficulty. Examples of these sorts of variables are negations, referentials, vocabulary, sentence length, number of paragraphs and so on. Different texts were then coded in terms of frequency of occurrence of each of the variables known to influence difficulty. Their analyses showed that quite a large number of these variables predicted item difficulty. They conclude that multiple choice reading tests are influenced by the same twelve categories of variables that have been shown to influence reading in the experimental literature. The findings are then taken as evidence for the construct validity of the multiple choice format for reading tests.

Freedle and Kostin present an interesting study using one approach to the issue of construct validity. We could argue that a different, but more direct approach, would be to gather verbal protocols from students as they attempt a range of different reading items. It may not be practicable to apply verbal protocol analysis to as large a sample as that used by Freedle and Kostin, but the approach would supplement their data and perhaps provide some direct support for their hypotheses. For instance, if students actually do find that negations, referentials, vocabulary (specifically the number of multisyllabic words) and so on increase difficulty, then this should be reflected in their behaviour. The incidence and length of pauses whilst reading could be taken to infer difficulty, as could re-reading.

Verbal protocol analysis can also play a useful role in gathering evidence to support the validity of inferences drawn from performance on novel assessments of reading. The written recall protocol is one of the newer ways of testing reading. Deville and Chalhoub-Deville (1993) note that the written recall protocol has at least two advantages over the more traditional tests of reading: (i) no clues about the content of the passage are provided, and (ii) the task requires candidates to construct as complete an understanding of the passage as possible. One of the difficulties with the written recall protocol appears to be the dearth of statistical evidence that would support its reliability. Deville and Chalhoub-Deville argue that without traditional item and reliability analyses, claims for the validity of the technique may not be made.

The written recall protocol is similar to an essay in that it comprises units representing recalled ideas about a text. The nature of these units and the links between them should correspond to the original text. Deville and Chalhoub-Deville found that upon carrying out item and reliability analyses, reliability estimates for the recall protocol were quite high. This suggests then that validation of the technique could usefully be attempted. The use of verbal protocols as part of this procedure could elucidate the cognitive processes underlying performance, and may also provide other information that could help in the selection of appropriate texts, for instance.

Finally, the methodology of protocol analysis may also be used to address questions of face validity and criterion relatedness. Face validity could be inferred using a similar procedure to that described above. Here, the focus would be the nature and content of task-related comments made by the test takers. A test that lacks face validity may well give rise to verbalisations indicating a problem. These might range from statements suggesting a general problem to more specific expressions of confusion about the test or aspects of it. Negative comments are clearly an indication of a problem but it is important to establish whether this problem is due to task difficulty, lack of motivation, or a poorly constructed test. Face validity becomes important when a superficial aspect of an assessment instrument interferes with candidates' performance.

Criterion relatedness is a rather different concern. Here, we are interested in the relationship between test scores and some criterion. The criterion behaviour may be performance on another test of the ability in question. If that is the case, then we are interested in the extent to which performance on our test correlates with performance on the criterion test. The criterion behaviour might be success in performing a task that involves the ability in question. In this case, we are likely to be interested in how well test performance predicts performance on the task in question. Criterion relatedness may be addressed in a number of ways. One approach involving verbal protocol analysis would be to use the same coding scheme to code protocols generated by test takers working on two different, but purportedly related, tests. A comparison of strategies used by students on both tests would allow inferences to

1 Verbal protocol analysis

be made about the relationships between the two tests. Tests which make similar cognitive demands should elicit similar sorts of processes from test takers. A similar approach might be used to assess predictive utility, the focus shifting from test to task. It is important to distinguish between test specific processes and those processes that underlie the ability in question. For this reason, coding schemes must be carefully developed to facilitate comparisons, especially if the tests involve different item types.

As can be seen from the discussion above, a range of the different validity questions may be addressed using fairly straightforward designs. Prepared sample materials might be presented to a representative group of potential test takers and either a concurrent or a retrospective procedure might then be used to gather the verbal protocols.

Writing

It is also possible to use the verbal report procedure as part of the validation process for writing tasks. Many of the same questions and approaches as described for reading would apply to validating inferences drawn from performance on various assessments of writing skills.

For instance, an existing assessment of writing skills in a foreign language might be evaluated in order to ascertain the degree to which the test measures both writing skill and knowledge of the language in question. Many assessments use writing tasks since writing is a means by which language skill and proficiency might be expressed. Writing skills are dealt with in detail in one of the worked examples presented in the following chapters, and so discussion here will be brief.

While reading tests frequently include well defined descriptions of good or correct responses, it is more difficult to achieve this for assessments of writing skills. Nevertheless, assessments of writing skills may be validated using a similar approach. For example, the UCLES' Certificate of Proficiency in English (CPE) requires candidates to complete two from a choice of five writing tasks. A description of the CPE writing paper and some example tasks taken from the UCLES' CPE Handbook are included in Appendix II.

One approach to the question of validating such an instrument might be to collect protocols from potential candidates as they attempt different versions of the same task. Assuming that the five different tasks assess the same basic skills, individuals who perform well on one task ought to perform well on variants of that task. Verbal protocol analysis then should help determine whether the five variants of the writing task all utilise the same classes of cognitive processes.

Another approach to validation might compare protocols collected from candidates completing this one task with protocols collected from the same candidates completing a related writing task. If the same skills are involved, this should be revealed, not just by statistical analysis, but more directly by the verbal protocol analysis.

Translation

Translation is similar to reading in that it calls for comprehension of a text, but thereafter the tasks diverge. In the case of reading, an understanding may be all that is required. Translation involves the additional processes of acting upon this understanding in order to reconstruct the target text with precision of meaning in another language, often the first language. Translation tasks may also be set in which the candidate is required to translate from their first language into a second language. The translation task L1 -> L2 is likely to be more difficult than the task of translating from L2 -> L1 since the former requires the generation of vocabulary and sentence structure in L1, whereas the latter requires the recognition of the counterparts of L2 words in the native language. Recognition is usually considered an easier task than the generation of the same information.

Hölscher and Möhle (1987) describe the ways in which a cognitive model of planning, developed by Hayes-Roth and Hayes-Roth (1987) may be applied to the analysis of translations. An interesting point made by their study is that individuals differing in level of skill in translation approach a translation task in very different ways. These differences may be captured by considering what goes on at different levels of planning. Furthermore, the processes involved in carrying out translation, and in this case, the planning processes, are revealed through the analysis of think aloud protocols. The same task then may elicit different cognitive processes from individuals differing in the extent to which they have developed the ability in question. As noted earlier, this is an important matter for our understanding of the term 'construct validity'.

How might verbal protocols be used as part of the validation of translation tests? One possibility might be in the selection of possible texts for use as part of an assessment of translation skill. Verbal protocols might be gathered from individuals differing in skill level as they carry out translations of different texts. This could reveal the extent to which the texts differentiate among the individuals, as well as allowing for more direct comparisons of texts. Finally, studies of individuals varying in skill level carrying out translation tasks should shed some light on the nature of skill in translation.

Verbal protocol analysis may be one of the few techniques which allows us to infer directly the range of cognitive processes underlying an ability, and more importantly, to specify the changes that occur in processing as the ability develops.

Listening

Listening shares some of the same skills as those involved in reading, with the obvious exception that the stimulus material is encoded through a different channel. While text may be returned to and re-scanned in the case of reading, an individual taking a listening test must rely on any notes made and recollections of the stimulus material. Buck (1992) argues that the skills involved in listening are sufficiently distinct from those involved in reading to justify measuring both separately. He used immediate retrospective verbal protocols and was able to gather quite a large amount of useful information on processes involved in listening.

Our discussion of reading referred to the study by Freedle and Kostin (1993) and their identification of factors known to influence reading difficulty. A similar approach might be taken for listening. Factors that influence listening difficulty may be inferred from candidates' behaviour as the test is carried out, and also through the analysis of protocols gathered retrospectively. For instance, Shohamy and Inbar (1991) used three different question types in their study of listening and found that questions testing local understanding were easier than questions testing for a more global understanding. These issues may be addressed using verbal protocols.

Verbal protocols might also be used to evaluate different forms of assessing listening skills. For instance, to compare different stimulus materials (conversations, radio recordings, and so on), and different test formats (multiple choice questions, true/false questions, note-taking, short answer questions and so on).

Summary

This chapter has described the methodology of verbal protocol analysis, considering issues surrounding its use and exploring practical applications for VPA in the context of language testing. We have seen that protocol analysis may play a useful role in the validation process, providing information that may more directly support interpretations from different test scores. Perhaps more significantly, protocol analysis may help elucidate the very 'constructs' that tests seek to measure.

Over the past fifteen years or so, the popularity and sophistication of protocol analysis have increased enormously. Many researchers are now satisfied that, when properly applied, the methodology can provide valuable and useful insights into behaviour, complementing other more quantitative approaches. In many instances, verbal reports provide a means for directly identifying and exploring the cognitive processes underlying performance on a range of tasks, processes which might otherwise only be indirectly inferred. In this respect, protocol analysis has much to contribute to the development and evolution of theories across a range of tasks.

The next three chapters describe in detail the procedure for carrying out protocol analysis in the domain of language testing.

2 Data preparation and collection

Introduction

This chapter deals with the following six issues in preparing and collecting data:

- task identification
- task analysis
- procedure selection
- using supplementary data
- data collection
- data transcription

In Chapter 1 we noted that many tests of language skill make use of one or more of the following sorts of assessment categories:

- reading
- writing
- translation
- listening
- speaking

In Chapter 1, some examples of validation questions that might be addressed using protocol analysis were described. The validation questions may be elaborated for the assessment categories described above and set in the context of the production and evaluation process. The production and evaluation process may be represented by Figure 5 below, taken from the Council of Europe's User Guide for Examiners in a Common European Framework of reference for Language Learning and Teaching (Milanovic 1997).

Verbal protocols may be used to help select, evaluate and modify materials and procedures. Verbal protocol analysis is likely to prove extremely useful during a number of phases of test development, including development of

2 Data preparation and collection

a specification and commissioning of material, selection and editing of material, trialling, pretesting and item analysis.

Figure 5:
Stages in the production of question papers
Development of a specification and commissioning of material

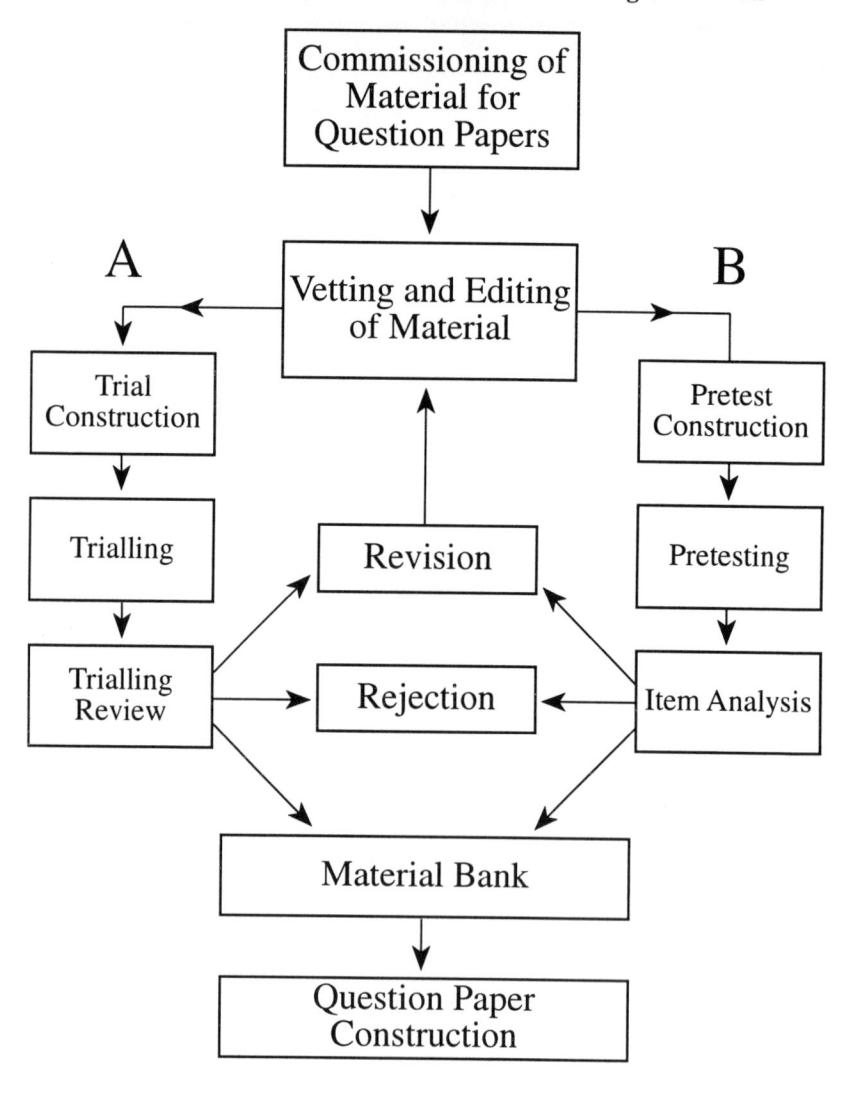

```
                    Commissioning of
                    Material for
                    Question Papers
                            |
                            v
        A          Vetting and Editing          B
        |          of Material
        v                  ^
   Trial                   |                Pretest
   Construction            |                Construction
        |                  |                    |
        v                  |                    v
   Trialling            Revision             Pretesting
        |                                       |
        v                                       v
   Trialling  ------>  Rejection  <------  Item Analysis
   Review
                            |
                            v
                    Material Bank
                            |
                            v
                    Question Paper
                    Construction
```

Verbal protocols may play a part in helping to specify the characteristics of the ability in question. For instance, Buck (1992) reports a number of studies of listening. Interviews with subjects revealed a number of characteristics of the skill that might not be revealed using less direct methods. Verbal protocols can help check that the ability in question has been appropriately described.

At the commissioning stage, a large quantity of material is generated and it is frequently not practicable to evaluate all this material using verbal protocols. Instead, poor quality material may be best filtered out during this early stage by experienced test developers.

Selection and editing of material

Strict guidelines should be followed in the selection and editing of material. Where guidelines do not exist to guide the selection and editing of materials, verbal protocols may supplement other information in the development of such guidelines. For instance, if guidelines are sought on the use of a particular item type, verbal protocols may be gathered to provide detailed information on the suitability of the item type. This might then inform test developers on the range of item types that are suited to the assessment category in question.

Trialling

Trialling is an important phase in the development of new tests since it is frequently at this stage that materials are first used in contexts closely approximating those of actual test use. Data are collected during trialling which are then analysed in order to filter out items or materials that are not functioning as anticipated. Protocol analysis can be invaluable at this stage, since it is often at trialling that unanticipated problems first surface. Verbal protocol data may supplement other quantitative data in order to determine characteristics of the items or tasks.

Verbal protocols can also be a good source of evidence in the construct validation procedure. It is worth pointing out that quantitative data cannot provide evidence on why a particular item does not function as anticipated, and cannot usually provide direct diagnostic information. Content analysis or verbal protocols may do this, allowing the test developer to pinpoint particular problems with a greater degree of accuracy. For instance, a particular passage may prove more difficult than anticipated as a result of the complexity of language within the passage, or because there is ambiguity in a question on the passage. The precise nature of problems such as these may be identified within verbal protocols. The information thus gained can usefully feed back into the test development process and into the training of item writers.

Pretesting

The purpose of pretesting is to allow items with known measurement characteristics to be banked, which allows new question papers to be generated, each with similar statistical properties. While verbal protocols facilitate the identification of poorly functioning items at the trialling stage, at pretesting verbal protocols may provide additional evidence as part of the construct validation process. In this case, the evidence may address a different aspect of construct validation, such as predictive utility or concurrent criterion relatedness.

Item analysis and evaluation

Item analysis provides information the test developer can use in considering which items to reject, whether revisions to items are required, and what those revisions might be. Data from verbal reports generated by individuals working on particular items, item types or materials can supplement information provided by formal task analysis. As we noted earlier, quantitative methods allow us to identify particular items, item types or materials that are not functioning well. They do not provide us with direct information on the nature of the problem. Verbal report data can provide more direct evidence on why an element of an assessment instrument is not behaving as anticipated.

Although evaluation is an ongoing part of the test development cycle, test developers may distinguish a separate and distinct phase of evaluation that occurs with item analysis. Evaluation is not particular to new tests, however, in that tests that are well established continue to be evaluated. At such an evaluation stage, verbal protocols can again play an important role. The sorts of questions that may arise at this stage can be more complex since other factors may become involved. For instance, marker or rater variables are generally involved in writing and speaking tasks. In the case of well established tests, evaluation may serve to address issues such as how to modify an instrument to make it easier to score, or to examine the impact of different marking procedures or criteria.

Summary

In the test development cycle then, the methodology of verbal protocol analysis may be used to address different aspects of construct validation at distinct phases of test development. A principal role is to ensure that the sorts of materials selected are geared towards the use of particular skills, such as reading and writing. Verbal protocols then may be used to justify the use of particular materials, and particular item types.

Verbal protocols can play a part in validating a new assessment technique, or a variation on an existing technique. Often, the impact of manipulating a task on performance cannot be predicted and it is necessary to trial. Verbal protocols can be used to allow comparisons to be made between performance on the new (or modified version) and performance on the test in its original format (or on a test which is assumed to measure the same skills). If the same skills are involved, this will be revealed in verbal protocols.

Points to note:

- Verbal protocol analysis may be used during a number of the phases of test development.
- Verbal protocols can help to evaluate materials, and can justify the use of particular item types.
- Verbal protocols can help identify the characteristics of items and tasks.
- Verbal protocols can provide valuable information to be used during the construct validation process.
- Verbal protocol data complement quantitative data that are routinely gathered as part of the evaluation process.

Task identification
Tasks

The most important initial consideration for the practitioner is whether or not the use of protocol analysis is appropriate for the situation or question in mind. We approach the issue of determining whether a task lends itself to protocol analysis by specifying attributes of tasks that render them suitable for protocol studies. We then go on to identify those aspects of tasks that are likely to render them unsuitable for protocol analysis.

First, what do we mean by 'task'? A task in this context refers to an activity that may be carried out by an individual, perhaps a test taker or an examiner. The task will usually be either to answer some questions making up a test, or to mark responses of subjects to test questions.

In deciding whether the task lends itself to investigation through protocol analysis, we need to specify the task attributes. Tasks that involve reading, listening, writing or speaking are generally suited to protocol analysis (although see earlier comments about special precautions that must be taken if VPA is to be used with listening and speaking tasks).

For the domain of language testing, we can be more specific and identify particular text and task types that may be used to assess a particular language ability.

The checklist below, which is derived from the Development and Descriptive Checklists for Tasks and Examinations produced by members of ALTE (Association of Language Testers in Europe), may serve as a useful guide. The checklist includes a range of different possible task types that are used to test the ability in question.

2 Data preparation and collection

Reading	Listening	Writing	Speaking
The types of text used might include:	The types of text used might include:	The types of task used might include:	The types of task used might include:
• Text from a book written for young adults • Newspaper article • Magazine article • Advertisement • Novel • Technical manual • Textbook • Bureaucratic document • Instruction leaflet	• Public announcements • Recorded messages • Weather forecasts • Traffic information • Tourist information • Publicity texts • Routine commands and instructions • Radio reports • Radio interviews • Vox pop • Conversations	• Free composition • Written task with text input • Summary • Expansion of notes	• Reading text aloud • Answering questions from the assessor • Problem solving • Discussion with assessor • Discussion with another candidate

Given that many tasks in an assessment context involve a considerable range of cognitive activities, it follows that a great many tasks are suited to examination through protocol analysis. With a wide range of tasks that are likely to be proved suitable, it is important to be aware of both individual and task variables that preclude the use of protocol analysis.

Unacceptable parameters of tasks

A number of factors may impact on the effectiveness of the VPA technique therefore invalidating it. Some of these are discussed briefly below.

• Guessing

Guessing should not be a principal means of responding. The reason for this is clear – protocol analysis is used to identify the sorts of mental processes and heeded information that are involved in carrying out particular tasks. True guessing involves selecting a response from a presented set, or from memory, when appropriate knowledge is missing. A verbal protocol generated by an individual who is guessing is very unlikely to shed any light on the sorts of knowledge and processes employed by an individual making a genuine

2 Data preparation and collection

attempt at the task.

For similar reasons, tasks which require Yes/No or True/False responses are unlikely to yield much useful information under verbal report conditions. Guessing might occur and so responses may simply be guesses rather than a reflection of knowledge. Alternatively, the individual may know the answer and generate the appropriate response. In either case though, it may be difficult to distinguish guessing from knowing, and this form of question does not encourage the individual to verbalise about any thoughts and heeded information involved in generating a response.

- Tasks which are too simple for the subjects in question

A second consideration centres on the skill level of the individuals producing the verbal reports. There is now a large body of data on skilled performance which suggests that as skill develops, performance becomes more highly automated and less subject to conscious control. In practice, this means that with skill development, what is verbalised may change. As noted in Chapter 1 in our discussion of translation skill, this may require a coding scheme that can accommodate differences in skill level. Automation of processing may speed up performance but makes intermediate products of processing unavailable to short term memory, and hence non-reportable. Verbal reports produced by individuals who have greatly automated processing for the task in question may not yield as much useful information as verbal reports produced by less skilled individuals.

Ericsson (1988) found that simple texts tend to be read with little additional information being verbalised. Difficult texts, however, slow down the reading pace, and give rise to much greater levels of verbalisation of additional information. In other words, problems may occur in the use of the verbal protocol analysis approach when the subjects are presented with what are, for them, very simple tasks.

- Speaking tasks requiring concurrent reports

Speaking tasks may not yield as useful and complete data under concurrent report conditions as under retrospective reporting conditions. This is because the typical speaking test requires the candidate to converse with an assessor, and a concurrent procedure would almost certainly disrupt this process. A retrospective procedure is one possibility if verbal reports are required for this class of task. This may be done by videoing interviews and asking assessors to retrospect very soon after finishing the interview.

- Perceptual-motor tasks and visual encoding tasks

Researchers have consistently found that tasks with a high perceptual-motor component and tasks which involve visual perception yield poor verbalisation.

Examples of perceptual-motor tasks include manipulation tasks. Highly visual tasks include judging a scene, describing a picture and drawing a picture.

Summary

We have seen in this section that many of the tasks typically used in language testing are suited to verbal protocol analysis. Often the issue is not identifying tasks that are suitable, but rather determining whether the task at hand lends itself to investigation using VPA.

Points to note:

- VPA may be used across a range of different tasks in the domain of language testing.
- Some attributes of tasks render them unsuitable for VPA.
- Care should taken in particular if VPA is to be used with speaking tasks.

Task analysis

As we have already seen, many tasks lend themselves to protocol analysis. We now consider what is involved in carrying out a task analysis.

A task analysis takes as its input the procedures, methods and knowledge that might be used in generating a response, analyses these and specifies a set of possible strategies. Where tasks are well defined and there is a consensus on what makes a correct or good response, the task analysis may be quite straightforward. For instance, Gerloff's (1987) study of translation skills uses well-defined syntactic units as a basis for the development of units of analysis for coding. These units include words, phrases, clauses, sentences and groups of sentences. These syntactic categories may be identified *a priori* and serve to shape the subsequent analysis. In this case, the task analysis is simplified since there is agreement on the definition of units and on the termino-logy (the syntactic categories, and the labels for such categories) used to describe specific chunks of text.

Where tasks are less well-defined, for instance in the case of examining, or written composition, then the task analysis may be more complex. In the absence of formal guidelines specifying what a unit might be, and detailing the kinds of strategies that are possible, the researcher must approach the stage of task analysis in a data-driven fashion. By this we mean that the researcher must decompose the task into its likely constituents and consider the different ways in which the task might be carried out. In the case of examining then, the task analysis might commence by specifying the information needed in order to carry out the task – this would include mark schemes, marking guidelines, question papers used by test takers, and the set of papers

2 *Data preparation and collection*

to be marked. This helps to define the vocabulary for the task, which is critical for the development of a coding scheme. Examiners might heed information from different sources and a poor task analysis may well yield weak categories that do not serve to highlight critical aspects of task performance. For instance, a task analysis that identified 'reading' as a behavioural category is likely to be far less effective than a task analysis that distinguishes among different types of reading (reading, re-reading, paraphrasing, and so on) or different reading materials (reading marking guidelines, reading the test taker's paper, reading the question paper, and so on).

In the marker strategies project used as an example in this book, a task analysis produced a tentative picture of the marking process. This is illustrated in Figure 6 below (Milanovic, Saville and Shen, 1996).

Figure 6:
A model of the decision-making process in composition marking

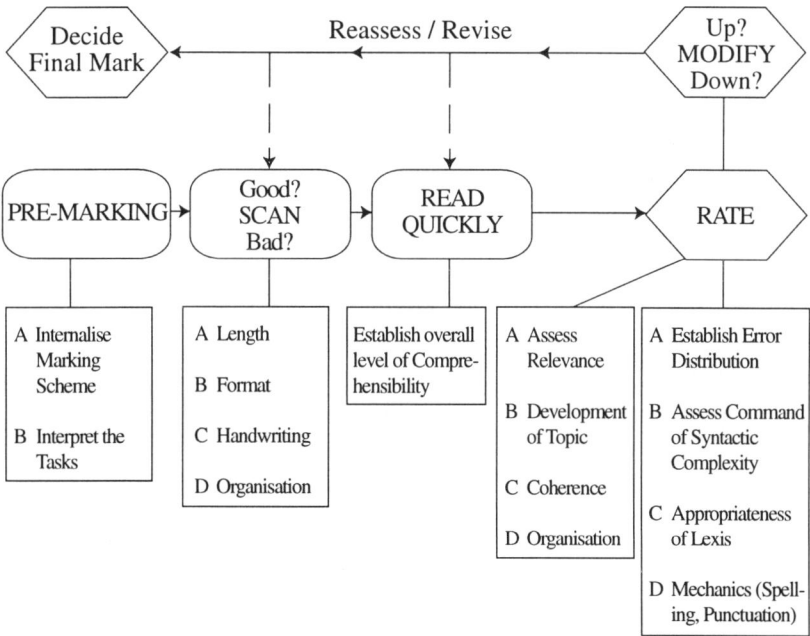

```
        Decide          Reassess / Revise              Up?
        Final Mark  ◄─────────────────────◄───────── MODIFY
                                                      Down?
            │              │          │
            ▼              ▼          ▼
                        Good?
      PRE-MARKING  ──►  SCAN   ──►  READ      ──►    RATE
                        Bad?        QUICKLY
            │            │            │          │          │
    ┌───────────┐  ┌───────────┐ ┌───────────┐ ┌──────────┐ ┌──────────────┐
    │A Internalise│ │A Length   │ │Establish  │ │A Assess  │ │A Establish Error│
    │  Marking   │ │           │ │overall    │ │  Relevance│ │  Distribution │
    │  Scheme    │ │B Format   │ │level of   │ │          │ │              │
    │            │ │           │ │Compre-    │ │B Develop-│ │B Assess Command│
    │B Interpret │ │C Handwriting│ │hensibility│ │  ment of │ │  of Syntactic │
    │  the Tasks │ │           │ │           │ │  Topic   │ │  Complexity  │
    │            │ │D Organisation│ │         │ │          │ │              │
    │            │ │           │ │           │ │C Coherence│ │C Appropriateness│
    │            │ │           │ │           │ │          │ │  of Lexis    │
    │            │ │           │ │           │ │D Organi- │ │              │
    │            │ │           │ │           │ │  sation  │ │D Mechanics (Spell-│
    │            │ │           │ │           │ │          │ │  ing, Punctuation)│
    └───────────┘  └───────────┘ └───────────┘ └──────────┘ └──────────────┘
```

One means of imposing structure upon less well-defined tasks, for the purposes of carrying out a task analysis, is to use a general purpose model of problem solving. If the task is seen as a 'problem' in a general sense, then attributes of the problem may be identified. These attributes should include the specification of an initial starting position or state (i.e. the problem or task), operators that may be applied to solve the problem (e.g. 'write'), task

2 *Data preparation and collection*

constraints (e.g., 'in no more than 350 words') and the goal or end state (i.e. an essay that answers the question in the appropriate way). The task analysis then might focus on the ways in which this might be achieved, given the particulars of the problem.

Points to note:

- A task analysis helps in specifying what is involved in carrying out the task in question.
- A task analysis provides information that helps in constructing a coding scheme later on.

Procedure selection

The previous chapter introduced the range of different procedures that may be used, with the recommendation that, as far as possible, concurrent reports are used. For language testing, we should note that the concurrent procedure may not be usefully applied with listening and speaking, and simple reading tasks tend not to yield detailed verbal reports. Beyond this though, the concurrent procedure may be used across a wide range of assessment tasks.

Deciding which procedure to use is quite straightforward. When retrospective reports are selected, some precautions should be taken. As we have already seen, retrospective reports must be gathered with care in order to avoid the possibility that additional information heeded after the task has been completed may be incorporated into the report. Provided the researcher is aware of these risks, then there may be situations where retrospective reports may be gathered more easily than concurrent reports.

Points to note:

- Concurrent reports are usually recommended.
- When retrospective reports are used, extra care must be taken.
- Both concurrent and retrospective reports may be used across a wide range of tasks.

Using supplementary data

It is sometimes useful to gather supplementary information, such as a videotape of the proceedings, or notes made by the individual reporting as the task was carried out. This may be used to clarify a verbal report and to facilitate the generation of the verbal report. In the first instance, notes made can disambiguate sections of report where it is clear that something is being referred

2 Data preparation and collection

to and there is uncertainty as to what it is. A video-recording of proceedings may be used in some contexts, especially oral interview situations, to facilitate the production of a retrospective verbal report.

Supplementary data should not take the place of the verbal report though. A sparse or incomplete verbal report should not be elaborated or made 'complete' by referring to supplementary data generated by the individual.

Occasionally, supplementary data may provide information that could not be inferred from the verbal report, for instance, duration of eye fixations and gaze direction. In the case of computerised tasks, supplementary data may take the form of a record of key presses made. This can be useful in revealing a candidate's first response and any revision of that response. Notes and other sorts of marks may also be used as supplementary data. Unless all individuals generate these data in addition to the verbal protocol, it may be simplest to allow the supplementary data to play a supporting role rather than to carry out full and extensive analyses on such data.

Points to note:

- Verbal protocols are a valid source of data in their own right.
- Verbal protocol data may be supplemented with additional information.

Data collection

The verbal reports generated by individuals under the different conditions (talk aloud, think aloud, concurrent, retrospective, mediated and non-mediated) constitute the data to be analysed. The most important consideration is to ensure that as much valid and complete data as possible are collected. The checklist below serves as a useful summary in the process of data collection.

Before the sessions

Preparation
Prepare clear and unambiguous instructions. Make sure you try them out on someone before working with subjects.

Briefing
Brief individuals on what is required of them, and explain the procedure that is to be used, i.e. think aloud or talk aloud, concurrent or retrospective reporting, probes or no probes.

2 Data preparation and collection

Practise the technique

Give individuals some practice tasks in order to familiarise them with the technique, and also to ensure that individuals are following the appropriate procedure rather than generating activity descriptions. Activity descriptions use the present progressive verb tense (e.g. 'I'm just reading this paragraph here', or 'I'm looking at this word here and wondering what it means'). Activity descriptions are not the same as thinking or talking aloud – activity descriptions are not prompted by instructions to think or talk aloud (although they may appear to be), but appear to be generated as a result of the individual prompting her/himself to describe what s/he is doing, or thinking about. Have individuals practise with both concurrent and retrospective reporting. Ericsson and Simon (1993) found that it is useful to have individuals practise with both forms of reporting when either a concurrent or a retrospective procedure is to be used. There are two main advantages to this:

(i) Having individuals generate both types of report emphasises the difference between concurrent and retrospective reporting.
(ii) The availability of both types of report allows the investigator to compare the contents of each. Both ought to contain roughly the same information.

Practise the task

If possible, provide individuals with practice in the chosen procedure on the task or tasks that will form the focus for the study.

During the sessions

Feedback

Provide feedback on thinking aloud or talking aloud performance so that individuals are aware of what is required and what to avoid.

Prompting

The instruction to 'keep talking' should be used if the subject falls silent for a period of time. This is less intrusive than 'Can you tell me what you are thinking?' and is less likely to encourage the subject to turn round to interact with the investigator.

2 *Data preparation and collection*

Time
Allow some extra time if the task under consideration has a fixed time limit, since the requirement to generate a verbal report can slow down performance.

Do not overextend
Restrict sessions to no more than one hour. It can be difficult to maintain concentration on the task, and to verbalise, for lengthy periods of time.

Equipment and venue

Equipment
Keep recording equipment as unobtrusive as possible. Cameras and microphones can be intimidating. Ensure that some practice is provided in the recording situation prior to commencing the data collection. It is well worth ensuring that the verbal reports are recorded on the best available recording equipment. Listening to the tapes afterwards is time consuming and the task can be made much more difficult if the recordings are of poor quality. The investigator will benefit from checking recording equipment and levels before gathering the verbal reports.

Venue
The recording should take place in a quiet room with few distractions. The investigator should not sit opposite or beside the individual who has been asked to generate the verbal report. This is to help reduce the amount of social interaction taking place and thus the amount of intrusion.

After the sessions

Debriefing
Debrief the subject at the end of the session and explain the purpose of the study.

Some instructions, with example practice tasks, for talk aloud and think aloud are given below. These are adapted from the instructions and practice tasks described by Ericsson and Simon (1993). Some example protocols are presented to illustrate the distinction between talk aloud and think aloud, and the difference between concurrent and retrospective protocols. The differ-

2 Data preparation and collection

ences between these procedures were described in detail in Chapter 1. In both the talk aloud and the think aloud examples, we show an example of a concurrent and a retrospective report.

Talk aloud

The first set of instructions are for use when the talk aloud procedure is required.

Some sample instructions for talk aloud, with practice tasks and sample protocols generated for the practice tasks, are illustrated below. The protocols are shown in italics.

> **Instructions:**
>
> In this study I am interested in what you say to yourself as you carry out the tasks I am going to give you. To do this, I am going to ask you to talk aloud as you work through the tasks. By 'talk aloud' I mean that I want you to say out loud everything that you say to yourself silently as you work through the tasks. It may help if you imagine that you are in the room by yourself. If you are silent for any period of time, I shall remind you to keep talking.
>
> Do you understand what I am asking you to do? Do you have any questions?
>
> We shall start with a few practice problems.
>
> First, I would like you to talk aloud as you multiply two numbers in your head. The numbers are 25 and 16.

2 Data preparation and collection

Sample concurrent protocol:

'OK so if I take four and multiply that by twenty-five, that gives me one hundred. Four fours are sixteen, so four times one hundred gives me four hundred. The answer is four hundred.'

Now I would like you to tell me what you can remember about what you did from the time you read the practice question until you gave your answer. I am interested in what you can actually remember, not what you think you may or should have thought. If possible, it would be best if you can tell what you remember in the order in which your memories occurred as you worked through the question. If you are not sure about any of your memories, please say so. I do not want you to try to solve the problem again, I just want you to tell me what you can remember thinking. Now tell me what you can remember.

Sample retrospective protocol:

'First I thought about getting easy numbers to multiply with. Then I noticed that four twenty-fives are one hundred. Then I saw that four times four equals sixteen, so I knew that I had to then multiply one hundred by four to give me the answer, which was four hundred.'

Next, I would like you to solve an anagram. I will show you a series of letters. Your task is to unscramble all the letters and to rearrange them to form a word in English. For instance, the letters O D O R can be rearranged to form the word DOOR.

Please talk aloud as you work on the following anagram. The anagram is:

$$E \quad W \quad R \quad A \quad T \quad S \quad E$$

Sample concurrent protocol:

'E W R A T S E. I'll try TER to start with. SWR – that doesn't make sense. RAT – I've used T and R though. SW – SWEATER, I've got it.'

Now tell me all that you can remember about your thinking.

Sample retrospective protocol:

'I just sort of looked at the letters and saw TER in there. Then I thought of SWR, but it didn't look like a word. The middle letters were RAT, but I was still thinking about the TER, and I saw I couldn't use the T and the R twice. Then I went back to SW and then got to SWEATER.'

2 Data preparation and collection

The concurrent protocol produced under talk aloud conditions shows the subject quite literally reporting all heeded verbal information. The retrospective report closely matches the content of the concurrent report, but the manner in which it is produced is quite different. The retrospective report takes place after the event and uses the past tense. It makes explicit the sequence of subgoals that have been set in order to solve the problem. The sequence of subgoals has to be inferred from the concurrent report. The retrospective report also contains a description of the strategy that was being used – identify numbers that are easy to manipulate, in this case, multiples of one hundred. Concurrent reports seldom explicitly report the strategy being used.

A task analysis of a simple multiplication problem such as this yields a number of different strategies that may be used in order to solve the problem. Each strategy predicts the information that will be heeded, and the order in which it will be heeded. We then compare the obtained sequence of reported information with that predicted by a particular model in order to infer the model that appears to have been used.

We contrast talk aloud with think aloud in the following section.

Think aloud

The instructions and practice tasks for the think aloud procedure are similar to those described for talk aloud. The think aloud procedure is most suited to tasks which may also involve non-verbal processes.

As in the example for talk aloud, some example instructions and practice

---

Instructions:

In this study I am interested in what you think about as you carry out the tasks I am going to give you. To do this, I am going to ask you to think aloud as you work through the tasks. By 'think aloud' I mean that I want you to say out loud everything that you are thinking from the time you start the task until you complete it. I would like you to talk constantly from the time you commence the task until you have completed it. It is important that you do not plan out or try to explain to me what you are thinking. It may help if you imagine that you are in the room by yourself. It is very important that you keep talking. If you are silent for any period of time, I shall remind you to keep talking.

Do you understand what I am asking you to do? Do you have any questions?

We shall start with a few practice problems.

First, I would like you to think aloud as you multiply two numbers in your head. The numbers are 25 and 16.

2 Data preparation and collection

Sample concurrent protocol:

'Well, if I set it out as a sum, I can see that six twenty-fives are one hundred and fifty. That leaves one to multiply by twenty-five and add a zero, so that's two hundred and fifty. Two hundred and fifty plus one hundred and fifty gives me four hundred. That's the answer.'

Now I would like you to tell me what you can remember about what you were thinking from the time you read the practice question until you gave your answer. I am interested in what you can actually remember, not what you think you may or should have thought. If possible, it would be best if you can tell what you remember in the order in which your memories occurred as you worked through the question. If you are not sure about any of your memories, please say so. I do not want you to try to solve the problem again, I just want you to tell me what you can remember thinking. Now tell me what you can remember.

Sample retrospective protocol:

'Well, I started by thinking of the numbers as you would a sum, so I multiplied twenty-five by six first of all, and that gave me one hundred and fifty. Then I did the next line, which was to multiply twenty-five by ten, adding the zero because that's what you do in multiplication. I got two hundred and fifty, then added that to the one hundred and fifty and that gave me four hundred.'

I would like you to complete some more practice problems. I would like you to do the same thing for each of these problems. I want you to think aloud as before as you work on the problem and once you have finished the problem, I want you to tell me all that you can remember about your thinking. Do you have any questions? I would like you to think aloud as you add up all the windows in your house.

Sample concurrent protocol:

'Well, starting upstairs there is one large bay window at the front, then on the landing there is one window, so that's two, go into the back bedroom and there's another, so three, then go into the baby's room and there's another, so four, then the bathroom makes five. Come downstairs and there's a window in the hallway. That's six. If I then go into the living room, there is a window there giving me seven.

2 Data preparation and collection

> *Coming out of the living room and going into the back room, there is a large french window, so that's eight. Then coming out of the back room and going into the kitchen there are two there, plus one in the pantry. So that's eight plus three, giving me eleven. There are eleven windows altogether.'*
>
> Now tell me all that you can remember about your thinking.
>
> **Sample retrospective protocol:**
>
> *'I started upstairs in the front bedroom, then imagined myself walking around the house and going into each room. So the hall is next to the front bedroom and it has a window, which gave me two. Next I went into each of the back bedrooms and added one window for each of them, making four. Then I went into the bathroom and added a window for the bathroom, so that was five. Coming downstairs there is a window in the hallway, so that gave me six. I went into the living room and added another, giving me seven. Next, I went into the back room and added the french window, so that was eight. Finally, I went into the kitchen and counted two there, plus the one in the pantry. I added three to eight and came up with eleven.'*

tasks are presented below with sample protocols shown in italics.

These protocols stand in contrast to those produced under talk aloud conditions. When we compare the protocols produced by the two individuals solving the multiplication problem under instructions to talk aloud and think aloud, we find evidence for different methods. The method reported under think aloud conditions suggests that a spatial representation is being used. We can deduce this from the fact that the individual first states that she will 'set it out as a sum', and then goes on to multiply as if she were working on a problem set out in the following way:

$$\begin{array}{r} 25 \\ \times\ 16 \end{array}$$

The sequence of heeded information in this case differs from that produced by the individual solving the problem under talk aloud conditions. We are therefore able to infer that a different model of multiplication has been used in this case.

Once again, the retrospective report corroborates the concurrent report in that there is a close match in information contained within both types of report. The retrospective report, referring to 'next line' lends further support to the idea that a spatial representation has been used in this case.

2 Data preparation and collection

Paired or individual reports

Under some circumstances, reports generated by two individuals working on a task can be useful and can serve to make explicit information that might not be apparent within a protocol generated by an individual working alone on a task. There is one principal problem associated with using this technique, and therefore we have only focused on individual reports so far.

The difficulty with paired reports is that the presence of another individual changes the way in which the task would be approached by an individual working alone on that task. Two individuals working together on a task interact, and each modifies the behaviour of the other. The manner in which the task is solved by a pair may differ enormously from the way in which either individual might solve the task alone.

Deciding whether to use a paired report procedure can be difficult. In deciding, it is worth considering the way in which the task would be carried out in an everyday situation. If the task is a test and the individual would normally work at this alone, then an individual protocol provides the closest fit with the real experience. If the task is examining, for instance, and examiners would usually work in small groups, then it may be worth considering a paired procedure. The difficulty of course with gathering and using verbal reports gathered from more than one individual is that more than one person may speak at any one time. This can complicate transcription and make it more difficult to preserve a record of the sequence of verbalisations.

Some examples of paired and individual concurrent reports are presented below. The first example was generated by a student working on translation, the second by two students trying to solve a mathematical problem.

Individual report:

> I'm trying to figure out – what does 'inhabituel' mean? They have ... they are not .... it is not usual. Um, next bit, what does that mean?

Paired report:

Student 1:	So, 'A cube has six faces. If each corner is removed by slicing off, how many surfaces does the cube now have?'
Student 2:	'If each corner is removed' – what does that mean? I can't picture it.
Student 1:	Well, if you slice the corners off, you create a triangular face where each corner was.
Student 2:	Oh, I get it – so that's the extra face. How many then? Six ...
Student 1:	No – you get four at the top of the cube and four at the base ...

Student 2: So that is eight, plus the six original faces, so fourteen altogether.

The individual report includes some evidence of self-prompting. ('What does that mean?') The paired-report procedure shows that the presence of a second person facilitates the generation of explanations of what is happening. The disadvantage however is that any inferences about behaviour have to be seen within the context in which that behaviour was produced, i.e. a social context. It would be inappropriate to generalise from the paired-report data and infer that individuals might behave in a similar way if acting independently.

Summary

Considerable care must be taken in briefing subjects on what is involved in producing a verbal report, as well as on what is required of them in carrying out the main task. The researcher should monitor events before, during and after the session to ensure that valid reports are produced.

Practice with both concurrent and retrospective reports can be very useful, and practice is essential if good verbal reports are to be produced.

Points to note:

- Good instructions are essential.
- Practice is important.
- Prompting may be necessary if silences occur.
- Collecting concurrent and retrospective reports during practice sessions can be a useful means of checking verbal reports.

Data transcription

The most lengthy part of the procedure is data transcription. While tapes may be transcribed by a skilled audio-typist, the researcher can learn a great deal through listening to the tapes. A written transcript cannot easily convey mood, tone of voice information, or pauses, for instance. Such prosodic and paralinguistic information can be useful and informative. Therefore, there are advant-ages to the researcher in carrying out some of the transcribing him or herself.

The transcriber should have access to any materials that were used or referred to as the protocol was generated. This is important because it is not always clear what is being said by the individual generating the report. For instance, background noise can mask part of an utterance. Alternatively, the individual might say something in a very quiet voice. Ambiguities such as these can sometimes be resolved by referring to the materials that were used at the time the protocol was generated.

Clarifying an utterance by referring to materials is quite different from the situation where the verbal report is for some reason incomplete. For instance, an individual might start a sentence and not finish it, or start a sentence, pause and then go on to refer to something else. This is illustrated in the following example:

040   'There is evidence that the cessation of advertising in ...'
041   So it looks as if the author is saying that ...
042   No, I think I'll read that paragraph again.
043   Oh – 'In 1963 the annual ...'

These three segments follow each other in sequence, yet two of the sentences are incomplete, and a certain amount of context is required in order to ascertain what is going on. Is the paragraph referred to in segment 042 the same as the paragraph that is actually referred to in segment 043? In this case, it is not, although this could not be apparent unless the researcher had the necessary materials to hand. Protocols should not be modified by adding or substituting words to achieve completeness, or by altering the verbalisation. Errors in language use then should be included in the transcript and should not be corrected.

Verbal protocols include a great many prosodic and paralinguistic elements, many of which are informative. It is therefore useful to develop a systematic approach to incorporating such information within the transcript. Pauses may be measured and indicated in the following way for instance:
'What do I have to do here?' [pause – 9 seconds]

Pauses often serve to mark segment boundaries. We shall return to this point in Chapter 4. A pause of some duration should meet with a prompt to 'keep talking'. Prompts should also be included within the transcript, and they should be highlighted so that it is clear that the prompt originated from the researcher, not the subject. This may be achieved by inserting any prompt on a separate line, apart from the text produced by the subject. A different font also serves to distinguish the subject's verbalisations from those generated by the researcher.

The length of the transcript, in terms of the number of words, may be contrasted with the length of the transcript in terms of duration. Time markers allow the researcher to compare how much has been said within a given period, and also to compare the extent of verbalisation within similar phases. We recommend that the length of pauses is captured. Marking regular intervals, such as ten-second intervals, is useful if an analysis of the length of time spent in

2 Data preparation and collection

carrying out different aspects of the task is to be examined. Intervals can be recorded by inserting a character within the text at the end of each interval.

The character used must be used consistently within each protocol and the same character should be used to code the set of protocols. The character used should not be one that might occur naturally within the text – thus letters, punctuation marks and mathematical symbols should be avoided. Some researchers have used characters such as '/' to indicate intervals. Whichever character is used, it must be distinguishable from the segment marker that will be used. We discuss segmentation in Chapter 4.

Once the set of protocols have been transcribed, the next ideal step is to check the transcripts against the original tape. This ensures that the transcripts are complete and accurate.

A final point to note is that data may require to be transcribed with care if the investigator is considering using one of the specially designed software packages for the analysis of qualitative data. Most packages require the data to be prepared in particular ways. The requirements of any package under consideration should be carefully noted prior to transcription, coding and analysis. For instance, a package may require that particular characters are used to denote segments and temporal intervals.

Points to note:

- Data transcription is a lengthy process.
- Protocols should be transcribed exactly as they are – they should not be tidied or altered.
- Care should be taken to ensure that any markers used are compatible with any software that may be used in data analysis.
- Non-verbal information may be useful, and where possible can be included in the transcript.
- Time markers should be used.
- It can be informative for the researcher to transcribe some protocols.
- At least some transcripts should be checked against the original recordings.

Worked examples

Two fully worked examples are presented below. The first describes the processes of analysing tasks, gathering and transcribing data for an assessment of students' L1 writing skills. The tasks involved here involve composition in the native language and much of what is said here will apply to other assessments of writing skills, and to assessments of L2 writing skills. The reader is taken through all the considerations made by the investigator in carrying out a task analysis, selecting an appropriate procedure, designing and carrying out the study and finally transcribing the data.

The second example focuses on protocols generated by a group of examiners assessing students' L2 writing skills, specifically in the context of the UCLES Certificate in Advanced English examination. The full study is described in the UCLES report, 'An investigation of marking strategies using verbal protocols' (Milanovic and Saville 1994). Again, the reader is taken through all the considerations made by the investigators in the preliminary stages of preparing and carrying out the study.

Example 1

L1 Writing skills

This particular study describes an approach to the issue of establishing validity for new assessment instruments, here two writing tasks. The aims were to examine the cognitive processes involved in carrying out two different writing tasks and to evaluate materials that were being prepared to assess the two different writing tasks. Verbal protocol analysis was chosen to elucidate the cognitive processes brought to bear on the tasks, to specify heeded information as the tasks were carried out and to facilitate comparisons between the two tasks and between different versions of the same task. The example begins by considering the nature of writing skills in some detail in order to identify the issues involved. This is important since writing is an ill-defined task.

The tasks that were the focus for this study were held to draw upon related but different skills. Task A, which is fully elaborated later, required individuals to read through some accompanying information on a given topic and to select, organise and present in written form information from this text relevant to the question. Task B required individuals to read an argument structured around a particular issue and to present a written evaluation of that argument, including where relevant further argumentation of their own.

Task identification and task analysis

Task identification in the case of this worked example was not a discrete phase because the tasks that formed the focus for the study had already been identified. It was therefore important to check that the tasks were suited to VPA. Since the tasks were both writing tasks, and writing tasks are known to be suited to VPA, the decision was taken to use VPA.

The task analysis begins by elaborating the strategies and processes that might be involved in carrying out these writing tasks. Tests of writing skills may appear to be different and may be structured around different materials, but they may require similar cognitive processes and strategies. Superficial

2 Data preparation and collection

differences among materials may mask underlying similarity. On the other hand, if the tasks differ along a number of significant dimensions, then different approaches should be required. One important factor then is likely to be the set of cognitive resources that are required in order to carry out a task.

Writing has two important facets: it requires thinking and it is a vehicle for thinking. If an individual can write well on a particular topic, we would tend to assume that s/he can also think effectively about that topic. This is a principal reason why performance on degree courses at universities is assessed by presenting students with a series of written composition tasks. Whilst it might be reasonable to suppose that good writing is a manifestation of skilled thinking, the position is a simplification and there are many more factors to consider if we are to understand what is involved in generating and evaluating a piece of written work. Our task analysis for writing skills must first consider the research that has contributed to our understanding of the nature and development of writing skills.

Expository writing is a task for which the goal 'emerges' (Scardamalia and Bereiter 1985). That is, the final piece of written work is constructed, shaped and modified as the individual works on the task. In general, writing is a task which requires the individual to bring to bear more information than is ultimately needed in order to complete the written piece. Thus, writing requires individuals to plan and co-ordinate their writing, access relevant knowledge, and monitor how the piece evolves. It is because there are obvious dependencies and interactions among these activities that Flower and Hayes (1980) argue that writing cannot be seen as a series of discrete and sequential activities. Writing imposes heavy cognitive demands in terms of the requirements for interactions between the different cognitive processes involved in planning, co-ordinating output and monitoring progress on the written piece.

The writing tasks with which we are concerned here differ from each other in a number of respects.

An example of Task A is presented below: (students were also provided with materials on the topic in question)

> **Task A**
>
> Task A does not require you to go beyond the information with which you are provided, for example, by providing additional information, by commenting on the facts or opinions provided, or by imagining that some readers might have particular needs beyond those specified; neither should you provide information which is not required by the task. You may find it helpful to separate the various texts from each other. You should also find it helpful to highlight, or underline, those parts of the texts which are relevant, before you start writing your answer.
>
> **Question**
>
> An article in your local newspaper suggested that, in order to save money, we should pull out of our involvement in Antarctica. Using the attached material, write an answer for the editor of the paper. You should explain the reasons for the British interest in the Antarctic – both past and present – and show how this interest has been made even more important by the Antarctic Treaty.
>
> **Time – one hour**

The test designer has hypothesised that Task A requires students to filter relevant from irrelevant information, to organise their selection and to present this. A number of strategies are possible. Students might attempt to read through all the materials first and then pass through them a second time, marking relevant text. Alternatively, students might mark relevant text on a first reading. A third possibility is that students might combine reading and selecting text with writing. Performing well on Task A depends critically on whether students are able to construct a good representation of the question, since the question guides the search for relevant text. Whichever strategy students adopt, they may successfully attempt the task by 'telling' what they know.

Task B, presented below, is very different (again, students were provided with materials on a particular topic). The test designer has hypothesised that Task B makes heavy demands on students' reasoning skills, specifically requiring them to evaluate an argument presented to them, and to generate further arguments. Possible approaches students might take here are likely to be quite different from those adopted for Task A. However, we should note that students may adopt something akin to the knowledge telling strategy for this task too. Knowledge telling might be triggered by an incorrect reading of the question, or by poor reasoning skills. We discuss knowledge telling later in the chapter. Students with poor reasoning skills might simply represent and describe the existing argument without any evaluation or additional argumentation.

Task B

Having read the following passage you should evaluate the author's argument and produce further arguments of your own in response to it.

By evaluation is meant looking at the way in which the author argues his or her case, including looking at any evidence which is used to support it.

In producing further arguments, you should go beyond what the author has said. You will need to think of arguments for both sides, for and against the author. What arguments can you think of which would support the author's case? What arguments can you think of which oppose the author? It is important that you show why these arguments are relevant, so give clear reasons why your further arguments are relevant to the theme of the passage. We are not assuming that one position is right and the other is wrong. You will be assessed primarily on your imaginative understanding and interpretation of the issue.

Your ability to write correct English is not the main concern with this exercise, but your answer should be clear and coherent.

Before you begin writing, read the passage and complete the summary exercise which follows.

Time – one hour

A consideration of writing tasks A and B indicates that both require processes involved in planning, accessing relevant information, co-ordinating this as written output and monitoring and evaluating. Evaluating processes must, in both cases, evaluate both given information and sections of text that are in the process of being written. Task A requires information to be evaluated for relevance, whereas Task B requires the argumentation presented within the given text, and the student's own further reasoning, to be evaluated.

Evaluating organisation and relevance of content of written text may be a focus in Task A. Task B requires the presented argument and any new reasoning to be evaluated.

We can begin to look at the requirements that each task makes on students and use these to guide the development of a coding scheme.

These task demands necessarily influence the development of the coding scheme. In evaluating writing, other factors will also play a role.

Any written piece might serve a number of purposes. It might provide an indication of how well an individual has assimilated information on a given

2 Data preparation and collection

Task A requires that students:	Task B requires that students:
read and interpret instructions	read and interpret the instructions (which in this case include the question to be answered)
read and interpret the question	
define the task	define the task
read and interpret the materials that are presented with the question	read the argument that is presented in the passage
determine which items of information are relevant	evaluate the reasoning presented
mark and select those items of information that are judged to be relevant to the task	summarise the reasoning
plan a response to the task	plan a response to the task
present the relevant material in a task-oriented fashion	select and evaluate arguments from the passage to support the student's own argument
	generate further arguments to support the student's own argument
evaluate the response to the task	evaluate the response to the task

topic. It can also show how well an individual can demonstrate their skill in writing, irrespective of the task that has been set. Performance of any individual on a writing task then is a function of several different factors:

(i)   the nature of the task set by the question setter
(ii) the knowledge and skills possessed by the writer
(iii) the knowledge and skills possessed by the assessor

There are several ways in which these representations of the task, which are constructed by each party, might interface. These are represented in Figure 7. Ideally, there should be a good correspondence (indicated by solid lines) between the task as represented by the question setter, the task as interpreted by the writer, and the task as interpreted by the assessor.

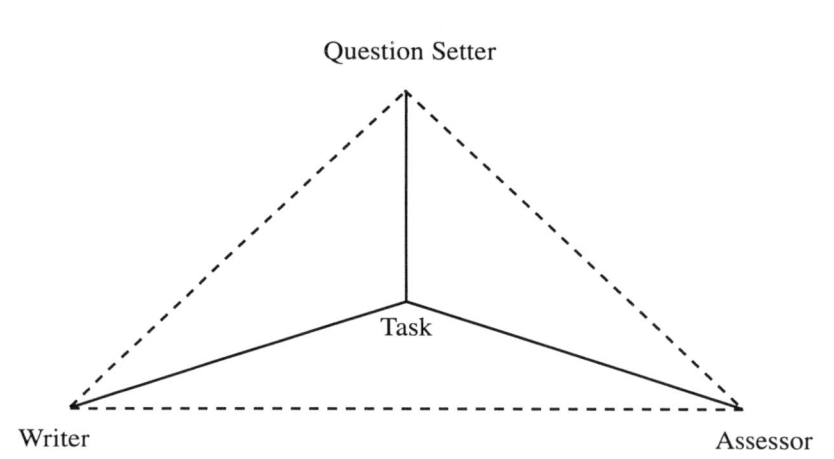

Figure 7:
Relationships between assessor, writer and question setter

```
                    Question Setter
                         /|\
                        / | \
                       /  |  \
                      /   |   \
                     /    |    \
                    /    Task   \
                   /      |      \
                  /_____|_____\
              Writer             Assessor
```

In practice, the mappings between the different representations are often less than ideal. The writer's representation of the task might be influenced by his/her beliefs on how the assessor or question setter sees the task. For instance, the student might attempt to answer the question s/he thinks the question setter posed rather than the question that has actually been posed. The experience of the question setter is likely to have some impact on the appropriateness of students' responses to the question.

Students are known to make the mistake of writing all they know on a given topic and adopting a 'knowledge telling' strategy rather than addressing the specific question that was asked (Bereiter and Scardamalia 1985, 1987). Bereiter and Scardamalia contrast knowledge telling with knowledge development. The latter is the more sophisticated strategy. However, knowledge telling may well suffice in order to carry out certain tasks. The wording of the question is an important factor in this respect. If the question setter wants the student to 'compare and contrast', 'illustrate with reference to examples', 'critically evaluate' and so on, then the question ought to contain words to signify this. These sorts of words should act as 'triggers', signalling that a knowledge telling strategy is not appropriate.

Independent of the students' representation of the task is the assessor's representation of the task. The assessor him/herself might misinterpret the question that has been set. This could manifest itself in the lack of agreement between markers, which is well documented (e.g. see Wood 1991) although not very well understood. (Rater reliability is the topic of the second worked example.)

Writing then is not a unitary skill – there are different types of writing (see Bereiter and Scardamalia 1987) and different sets of cognitive processes configure in order to meet the demands of various writing tasks. Similarly, the ability to score or grade a piece of writing is not a unitary skill – it requires processes of comprehension, interpretation and evaluation. In both cases, the definitions of a 'good' piece of writing and 'good' examining tend to be rather subjective. Decisions are typically made about attainment or aptitude on the basis of one individual's assessment of a piece of writing. Again, these sorts of issues are taken up when we move on to consider the second worked example.

Procedure selection

Of the different procedures that might be used, concurrent protocols are best used wherever possible. In the case of both writing tasks, the think aloud procedure was selected. Task A required students to comprehend verbal and non-verbal material, and thus the talk aloud procedure would have failed to capture non-verbal thoughts.

In developing the test materials, certain inferences had been made about which skills each instrument assessed and about how students would respond to the different tasks. The principal objective was to examine the extent to which these assertions were justified. The second objective was to identify the sorts of strategies that skilled and less skilled writers use. Third, it was hoped that the study would allow an evaluation of the two sets of different materials used to assess performance on the writing tasks.

The study

Eight students (three males and five females) each completed one Task A essay and one Task B essay. Students were drawn from a variety of backgrounds and were specifically selected as representative of the target group of users of the writing tests.

The students were asked to think aloud as they worked on the essays. The protocols they generated were concurrent protocols. Instructions to think aloud were drawn from Ericsson and Simon (1993). Each student was tested separately and each was given time to acquaint him/herself with the task and with the think aloud procedure. When students were clear about what was required, they were asked to proceed with the task. Students were prompted to continue talking if they fell silent at any stage. A time limit of one hour and fifteen minutes was imposed on each task. An extra fifteen minutes was allowed to compensate for the effects of having to talk as the task was carried out. Students were notified towards the end when there were ten minutes, and then five minutes remaining.

The scripts were marked by an examiner trained in marking these particular types of essay. The two different classes of essay were marked according to two different sets of criteria.

For Task A, the criteria were:

(i) The ability to select relevant from irrelevant material.
(ii) Organisation, clarity and register – the abilities to organise a response, and to present it clearly and in the appropriate register.

For Task B, the criteria were:

(i) Critical evaluation – the ability to evaluate critically the argument that has been presented.
(ii) Further argumentation – the ability to produce relevant further argumentation.

Data transcription

Data from each of the tapes were transcribed in full. As expected, students took a little longer to complete each essay than they might have done had they not been asked to think aloud. Time markers were not used in this study. The main focus for the study was to identify the processes and strategies used by students rather than to carry out a more detailed analysis of time spent on each phase of activity.

The transcripts quickly revealed that students had been able to think aloud as they carried out the task, and the frequency with which students verbalised activity descriptions was very low.

Example 2
Marker Strategies in Assessing CAE Compositions

The aims of the second example were to identify marking strategies examiners use and to evaluate the adequacy of the marking guidelines. These aims were part of a broader initiative which aimed to increase the reliability of marking written work. A number of studies have shown that different examiners respond to different aspects of writing (Diederich, French and Carlton, 1961). A study by Grobe (1981) suggested that examiners are greatly influenced by the diversity of vocabulary used in the written piece, while another study by Freedman (1979) found that content was the most significant factor in arriving at a final evaluation of an essay. A study by Stewart and Grobe (1979) showed that examiners may be influenced by length and accuracy. Milanovic and Saville (1994) conclude that examiners do not appear to be measuring a single common construct in evaluating written work. Of course, as we noted in the previous example, writing is probably best seen as a product of a cluster of skills than as a single ability.

Some specific questions were of interest to the researchers in this example:

(i)   Is it possible to abstract a model of good marking behaviour?
(ii) What distinguishes good examiners from poorer examiners?
(iii) What influences rater consistency?
(iv) Do raters adjust their marking behaviour according to the level of the script?

Task selection and task analysis

Since the task for examiners involved evaluating and marking written work, a number of points had to be considered in selecting an appropriate assessment task. To provide as much useful information as possible on examiners' marking strategies, the most basic tests of writing were excluded. These were unlikely to be evaluated using as wide a range of criteria as the more advanced assessments. An earlier study by Milanovic, Saville and Shen (1992) had focused on examiners' strategies while marking First Certificate in English (FCE) compositions and Certificate of Proficiency in English (CPE) compositions. The study described here selected a relatively new examination, the Certificate in Advanced English (CAE). The earlier study carried out by Milanovic *et al.* (1992) had suggested a number of different marker strategies that might be adopted. A model of the decision making process in composition marking, based on these initial studies, had been constructed. Of interest was the extent to which this model might generalise to the marking of other compositions, in this case, to the marking of CAE paper 2 compositions.

The task analysis begins by considering the nature of the task students had been set, the strategies examiners have been shown to use when reading and marking other compositions and the criteria examiners are asked to use in marking CAE compositions.

Students were asked to write two essays. The essays were to be based on some information provided. This information is reproduced below.

Milanovic *et al.* (1992) describe four different strategies used by examiners when marking CPE and FCE compositions. These strategies were inferred from examiner responses to questions about marking behaviour.

- Principled two scan/read – read twice before deciding on a final mark.

- Pragmatic two scan/read – read twice for a specific purpose before deciding on a final mark.

2 Data preparation and collection

- Read through – read once and decide on a final mark once the script has been read.
- Provisional mark – make an initial assessment while reading and continue reading to confirm or alter the initial assessment.

The task:

> A fortnight ago you were on holiday in Scotland. One evening you went to the cinema with a Scottish friend of yours, called Malcolm Taylor. On the way home together, you witnessed an attempt by a young man to steal a woman's handbag. Malcolm tried to help the woman, and although the thief managed to run away, nothing was stolen. Malcolm suffered a bad cut to his face. You have just received the letter below from Malcolm with the newspaper cutting enclosed.
>
> Read the letter and newspaper cutting and then, using the information carefully, write the letter and note listed on the next page.

... It was great to see you last month. I'm glad you enjoyed your holiday – back at work now I suppose – hope it's not too boring! The reason I'm writing is to ask you a favour. If you read the enclosed, you'll see it's supposed to be a report about that incident outside the Rex Cinema, I'm sure you'll remember it. Anyway, as you can see, they've given the impression I was the mugger! Whether it's just bad reporting or they've missed a paragraph I can't make out, but the facts are all wrong – even your nationality. Typical!

I've phoned them and they say they'll print a correction, but I know that just means a sentence hidden away at the bottom of one of the back pages.

Would you mind writing a letter to the paper, saying what really happened?

I think they'll print it if you've taken the trouble to write from abroad. I'd be really grateful – all my family's friends read this local paper and the report really makes me look bad.

Many thanks. Keep in touch, hope to see you again soon.

Malcolm

Handbag Thief Caught

A YOUNG MAN was arrested outside the Odeon Cinema in Grant Street last Thursday after attempting to snatch the handbag of a woman passer-by.

Malcolm Taylor, 24, a Eweness resident, was accompanied by an American tourist who was not, however, involved in the incident. Miss Erskine, 27, suffered a cut to her face and was badly shaken. She said she was most upset by such an incident happening in a place like Eweness, but added "I'm really most grateful to my rescuer."

Write   (a)   the letter to the Eweness Weekly Times as requested by Malcolm (approximately 200 words)

(b)   a relevant note to Malcolm (which you would attach to a copy of the letter) (approximately 50 words)

You must lay these out in an appropriate way but it's not necessary to include an address.

The criteria examiners are asked to use in carrying out first impression marking of CAE compositions are described in Table 1.

Three factors help to specify the range of different approaches that examiners might adopt, and the different categories of information that might be heeded during the marking of a student's composition. Misperception or misinterpretation of the question is likely to be one factor contributing to between-rater disagreement. Variations in familiarity with the task and/or materials, and differences in marker experience are two other factors which might influence reliability of ratings.

2 Data preparation and collection

Table 1:
Marking criteria for UCLES Certificate in Advanced English

Level	Criteria
5	Totally positive effect on target reader. Minimal errors: resourceful, controlled and natural use of language showing good range of vocabulary and structure. Completion of task: well organised, good use of cohesive devices, appropriate register, no relevant omissions.
4	Sufficiently natural, errors only when more complex language attempted. Some evidence of range of vocabulary and structure. Good attempt at task, only minor omissions. Attention paid to organisation and cohesion; register not always natural but positive effect on target reader achieved.
3	Use of English satisfactory though lacking variety and range. Occasional serious errors should not impede communication although patience required of reader. Task reasonably attempted with some organisation and cohesion; no significant irrelevancies.
2	Errors sometimes obscure communication and/or language too elementary. Some attempt at task but notable omissions and/or lack of organisation and cohesion could have negative effect on reader.
1	Serious lack of control and/or frequent basic errors. Narrow range of language. Totally inadequate attempt at task.
0	Not sufficient comprehensible language for assessment.

Not all individuals agree on what constitutes 'good writing' and thus evaluating a written piece may be considered an ill-structured task. Explicitly evaluating a writer's skills requires a rater who then applies some assessment criteria. The ability to make an assessment of a written piece is itself a cognitive skill which requires the assessor to think effectively. The assessor might reward a writer on the grounds of information presented in the written piece irrespective of how well that information is organised and presented. Alternatively, the assessor might award points for evidence of good thinking – layout, structure, coherence and sound argumentation. In some cases, an assessor might have to consider both simultaneously. For many tests and examinations, examiners receive little by way of formal training. Instead, they are usually asked to use their domain knowledge to make judgements about the performance of candidates. It is often found however that the biggest source of error is attributable to differences between markers. What can a study of observed marking behaviour tell us about marker strategies, and can it inform us on how best to train examiners so as to reduce rater error?

A task analysis for the purposes of this study then showed that markers might use one or more of the strategies identified. In evaluating the compositions, markers should refer to the mark scheme and use the marking criteria. It is of course possible that other criteria might be used too, and so the coding scheme should accommodate both task relevant and any task irrelevant criteria.

Markers were set the task of marking twenty CAE compositions. Each examiner was given the same compositions arranged in one of four different orders and numbered from 1 to 20. Mixing the order of presentation of the scripts is a basic design principle borrowed from experimental psychology. Order effects are known to influence performance on tasks. The same may well be true for the task of marking essays. Order effects were minimised by adopting the four different sequences of presentation. Examiners were asked to mark the essays in a single session and to mark them in the order presented to them. Each script was awarded a score on a scale of 0 to 5 and each score was recorded on a mark sheet. Examiners prepared a retrospective written report after marking and completed a short questionnaire. These latter two tasks served to gather up additional information about the marking and about the examiners that might not be apparent from the think aloud protocols alone.

Procedure selection

The concurrent think aloud procedure was used. Think aloud rather than talk aloud was used because raters may comment on non-verbal aspects of a composition, in particular aspects such as text layout and handwriting quality. Concurrent rather than retrospective reports were selected in order to reduce the likelihood of additional information being incorporated into the protocol after the marking event.

While experienced, the examiners who took part in this study had not before been asked to think aloud as they marked exam scripts. Examiners were carefully trained in the think aloud procedure. As pre-training preparation for the study, each of the examiners was sent two CAE scripts for marking. Examiners were asked to record onto a cassette tape all their thoughts at the time of marking the scripts. The study was designed so that marking would be carried out at home. The pre-training preparation gave an indication of what examiners understood by think aloud. This varied considerably from examiner to examiner and showed clearly that a formal training session was needed. On the basis of the initial instructions, some examiners had generated very sparse protocols which had all the hallmarks of activity descriptions. Other examiners went to the opposite extreme and generated extremely full protocols. The difficulty with the very elaborate protocols was that examiners did not usually spend so long marking a script. The instructions to think aloud then had been mistaken for 'say as much as you can about the following two sample scripts'. Both of these scenarios are to be avoided in practice, and training is the best way to achieve this.

Examiners were invited to attend a training session. At the training session, examiners listened to an introductory talk which explained the aims of the project and went into some detail about the think aloud procedure. Examiners then separated into groups and were given instructions and practice in thinking aloud, in addition to feedback on their own first recorded attempts at thinking aloud. The training session ensured that all examiners knew what was required of them and that they had each had some practice with the think aloud procedure. This is likely to be extremely important in contexts where individuals asked to generate verbal reports do so alone and without supervision. It is not always practicable to have individuals generate protocols under supervision.

Data transcription

Cassette tapes were returned to Cambridge once marking had taken place. Data from each of these tapes were transcribed in full. The data were transcribed by an audio-typist. The researchers listened to the tapes and checked the transcriptions.

Summary

The two worked examples illustrate the use of verbal protocols in two quite different settings. Important issues are raised by each study.

Study 1 shows that a task analysis and an emphasis on the cognitive processes involved in writing can contribute to an understanding of what it is that different composition tasks demand. This can be used to help check the specification developed by the test designer.

Study 2 shows the importance of careful training in the appropriate procedure. Simply providing the examiners in this study with instructions on how to think aloud was not sufficient – a formal training session was needed in order to ensure that each examiner understood what was meant by think aloud and to ensure that each examiner had learned to think aloud.

Summary

This chapter began by discussing the possible uses of verbal protocol analysis as part of the test development and evaluation process. Once the methodology has been identified as appropriate, questions to consider centre on the task analysis and selecting the best procedure for the application in mind. These questions are not trivial, as the two worked examples revealed.

Having decided on a procedure, a good deal of care must be taken to ensure that what is generated is a valid verbal report, and to minimise the possibilities of distortion or alteration of heeded information.

Tutorial exercise

In this section we present some task materials and marking criteria. In this case, we are interested in a comparison between two different but related tests of reading. Do the tests measure the same underlying ability?

The purpose of the exercise is to select an appropriate procedure for gathering verbal reports and to carry out a brief task analysis, which will form the basis for coding a set of verbal protocols. Some guidance is provided in Appendix III.

3 Developing a coding scheme

Introduction

This chapter focuses on the decisions and procedures involved in developing a coding scheme to analyse the gathered verbal protocols. By the end of the chapter, the reader should have an understanding of the issues involved in coding verbal protocols and should be in a position to try out the tutorial exercise that follows the worked examples.

One of the main points to make at the outset is that there is little consensus on the precise nature of the coding categories that may be used for the analysis of verbal report data. This is partly due to the existence of more than one model to account for cognitive activity in a number of domains. Reading is a good example in that there are a number of different models of reading. Two researchers may independently develop different schemes for the analysis of the same body of data. This does not invalidate the technique, but rather affects the inferences that may be drawn following different analyses. We elaborate below on some of the issues involved. Our purpose here is not to prescribe to the reader some coding schemes that may be used for different applications in language testing but to elaborate on the factors that should be considered for the development of coding schemes.

Researchers may differ in their choice of coding categories for analysing protocol data. At the simplest level, the choice of labels for coding similar segments may vary from researcher to researcher. Coding schemes may also differ in granularity and power. For instance, a coding scheme that comprises a small number of broad coding categories may allow the researcher to make only very general, and perhaps weak, inferences. A coding scheme that comprises more categories may allow the researcher to make more specific inferences. However, coding schemes that use a small number of categories tend to result in higher levels of inter-coder agreement, and so may be said to be more reliable. Coding schemes which use a larger number of categories can be more difficult to use if the coding categories are not sufficiently distinguishable, and hence often give rise to lower levels of inter-coder reliability. Inter-coder reliability is considered in Chapter 4. First we tackle some of the issues central to the development of a coding scheme.

Developing a coding scheme

One of the issues to consider in developing a coding scheme is the relationship between what are termed task-independent process categories and performance on the task in question. Ericsson and Simon (1993) review a large number of studies which have attempted to code protocols in terms of largely task-independent processes. They conclude that little has been learned about cognition from studies of this nature. The difficulties lie with some assumptions that are made, either explicitly or implicitly, by direct approaches. One assumption centres on the role of general processes, and a second assumption concerns segmentation of protocols. Direct approaches assume that evidence for general processes predicted by a particular theory may be found in the protocol. Direct approaches base segmentation on the identification of instances of such processes within the protocol. As we shall see in the following sections, neither assumption is well founded.

An example of a direct approach in the case of language testing might be to construct a theory of processes involved in reading comprehension and then to use this theory to identify a set of process categories to code verbal protocols generated by individuals carrying out a range of tasks which include reading and comprehending. Although a crude example, it should be obvious that to generalise a theory in this way is likely to be inappropriate. Tasks that require reading and comprehending may require other processes too, and these other processes would not be captured by an encoding in terms of task-independent processes. Thus, the coding of verbal protocols should commence by focusing on heeded information contained within the protocol. It is this information that is likely to reveal the processing that has taken place.

Developing a coding scheme for the analysis of verbal protocols involves the construction of categories that best capture the information heeded as the verbal protocol was produced. Coding the protocols then becomes a matter of matching each verbalisation with a category that captures the same information. For instance, the following four statements are excerpts from a protocol produced by an examiner thinking aloud as she marked a student's piece of work. The task was to read some background information and then to write a short letter based on the background material.

005   'Well, it's set out like a letter.'
017   'That's the wrong register.'
036   'I really don't think it's answering the question.'
041   'I think I would give her 3 for that.'

It is quite clear that the numbered segments each refer to a different aspect of the marking task. In segment 005, the examiner is conducting an overview of the visual appearance of the letter. In segment 017, she has commenced

3 Developing a coding scheme

reading the student's letter and has detected a problem with the appropriacy of the language used. Later on at segment 036, the examiner gives an evaluation of whether the student has responded appropriately to the task as a whole. Finally, segment 041 is the mark decision.

Keeping any theoretical assumptions to a minimum, we may begin to think about a coding scheme that captures the range of heeded information that is illustrated in the protocol segments given above. Segments 005, 017 and 036 describe different aspects of the writing that are being noted. The full protocol also includes references to spelling and grammar. The coding categories that could be used to code this protocol then might include categories to distinguish between the different features of the letter that have been noted by the examiner. A further set of categories may capture evaluations that are made by the examiner. For instance, segment 017 includes a negative evaluation of the appropriacy of language.

Other categories would be required to capture the decision-making behaviour of the examiner. Segment 041 simply states the final mark the examiner makes for the piece in question. Decision making can be quite complex, though; and other examiners may use rather different approaches. For instance, a different examiner rating the same piece of work as described above produced the following statements:

039   'This is better than the last one.'
040   'I'll give this one 3.'

These segments illustrate decision-making behaviour, but we can see that it is rather different from that used by the first examiner above. Here the decision making appears to be normative.

In the introduction to this chapter we noted that coding schemes can be a result of adopting *a priori* a particular model or theoretical framework. A problem associated with this approach is that hypotheses consistent with the particular model or theory, rather than those that are inconsistent, tend to be tested. It is good practice in protocol analysis to develop coding schemes that allow for testing both classes of hypothesis.

Another reason why coding schemes should allow for testing multiple hypotheses about the ways in which individuals might approach tasks is that individuals differ along a number of dimensions, amongst which experience, ability and motivation are likely to have a significant impact on performance.

The main purpose of the coding scheme then is to capture as much of the information within the set of protocols as possible. Coding categories should be quite specific. At the same time, though, coding categories must be generalisable across a number of protocols in order to allow for comparisons among individuals who have completed similar or identical tasks. A good coding scheme achieves a balance between specificity and generalisability. Poor

3 Developing a coding scheme

coding schemes can be either too general, failing to capture adequately the cognitive activity involved in carrying out a task, or too idiosyncratic and thereby failing to represent typical behaviour.

Highly detailed coding schemes can sometimes result when a scheme is developed with reference to just one or two protocols. The temptation is to decompose categories into sub-categories, each of which more accurately seems to capture the information in the segment. These schemes may describe a small number of protocols very well, but their weaknesses can become apparent when efforts are made to use them to code larger sets of protocols. It can be difficult to match specific categories with the range of utterances that typifies most verbal protocols. Coding schemes that give rise to a great many specific categories also tend to be less reliable, a problem we return to in Chapter 4.

Recall that each segment should represent a single process, such as 'read' or 're-read'. Many researchers are interested in the range of different strategies that are used to carry out tasks rather than the constituent processes. It is important to consider how strategies are inferred from verbal protocols, and how they are represented by different coding schemes.

An individual strategy can be considered as a unique sequence of processes. Thus, strategies are inferred from verbal protocols by examining the protocols for particular sequences or patterns of processes. The strategies may be defined *a priori* or the protocols may be coded and strategies inferred after coding. We discuss a hypothetical situation below.

Example

Two French students are presented with a reading comprehension task in order to assess their English language skills and to explore the sorts of strategies they might use. They are asked to think aloud as they work through the task.

Student 1 generates a protocol, part of which is coded as follows:

001	Read (English)
002	Re-read (English
003	Read (English)
004	Re-read (English)
005	Read (English)
006	Focus (English)
007	Retrieve (French)
008	Read (English)
009	Read Question 1 (English)
010	Re-read Question 1 (English)

3 Developing a coding scheme

011 Re-read (English)
012 Re-read Question 1 (English)
013 Scan (English)
014 Read Question 2 (English)
015 Re-read Question 1 (English)
016 Respond (English)

Student 2 generates a different protocol, part of which is coded as follows:

001 Read (English)
002 Focus (English)
003 Re-read (English)
004 Read (English)
005 Focus (English)
006 Re-read (English)
007 Read Question 1 (English)
008 Focus (English)
009 Keyword search (English)
010 Respond (English)

    The two extracts above are used solely to illustrate a few very simple points. The reader should note that neither example, nor the descriptions of them below, is used to support a particular model or theory of reading comprehension.
    We begin by considering Student 1. From the coded segments, this student appears to go through a cycle of reading followed by re-reading sections of the passage. At segment 006 the student 'focuses', perhaps on a particular word or phrase, and then retrieves the meaning of that particular word or phrase. This could suggest an initial failure to understand and then retrieval of the appropriate meaning. The student then reads the question, re-reads the question and then re-reads some text. Further cycles of re-reading the question and the text then ensue before the question is answered.
    Student 2 approaches the task differently. Student 2 reads a section of text, focuses on a phrase or word and then continues to read. The cycle is repeated until the passage is read. Responding to the first question on the text, the student reads the question, focuses on a particular word or phrase and then searches the text for that word or phrase. The question is then answered.
    The major point made by these two extracts is that although both students use similar processes, the pattern of processing, and thus the strategies used, differ. The pattern in each case is interrupted at key points – for instance, Student 1 goes on to read Question 2 before returning to Question 1 – but nevertheless, a pattern is discernible.

3 Developing a coding scheme

Our hypothetical researcher might also wish to consider a range of other questions. Are there links between the different patterns of activity and performance on the task? Is there anything in the protocols to suggest that difficulties with the task are due to the materials rather than to the students' lack of ability?

Developing a good coding scheme is critical to abstracting useful and valid information from verbal protocols. The coding scheme shapes and constrains the inferences that may be drawn from the data. In the next section we consider the units for analysis and the nature of the segments that are to be coded.

Points to note:

- The coding scheme must enable as much of the information within the protocols to be captured as possible.
- Theoretical assumptions should be kept to a minimum.
- The coding scheme should enable the researcher to test hypotheses that are both consistent and inconsistent with a particular approach.
- The coding scheme should allow for individual variation in how tasks might be carried out.

Identifying the main unit for analysis

A unit for analysis will usually comprise a phrase, clause or sentence. Phrases and sentences are delineated in speech by pauses, intonation and so on. These natural contours should also act as markers for segmentation of the verbal protocols. Approaches that focus on the identification of general processes within the protocol would naturally take an instance of a particular general process as a segment. The difficulty here is that the general process may correspond to a fairly large chunk of protocol. For instance, if we assume that a general process in rating a piece of written work might be to note the overall structure and layout of the written piece, marking paragraphing, the length of the piece, and so on, then the segment may be quite large. Other activities that occur within the segment may be masked and indeed lost if the segment is simply coded as an instance of the general category of 'overviewing'. It is also questionable whether a broad category such as 'overviewing' is representative of a single process or in practice might subsume several processes. As we noted above then, this approach is problematic and has little to recommend it.

For some tasks, the size of the unit for analysis can be particularly informative. For instance, the size of the unit for analysis for translation tasks can provide information on how translation skills develop. Gerloff (1987) describes a study which used think aloud protocols to identify both the unit

3 Developing a coding scheme

for analysis in translation and the range of strategies used by individuals carrying out translation work. To begin, Gerloff developed a seven level scheme for coding the unit for analysis. These seven levels were:

Level 1 – morphemes or syllables as units
Level 2 – words as units
Level 3 – phrases as units
Level 4 – clauses as units
Level 5 – sentences as units
Level 6 – two or more sentences as units
Level 7 – non-syntactic groups as units

Analyses of protocols generated by six individuals showed that much of the processing activity occurred at these levels, and that the pattern for individuals varied. Some individuals approached translation tasks by focusing at the level of words and phrases, while others worked with sentences as their main unit. An analysis in these terms is important because, in the case of translation, it allows for an examination of possible skill-related differences in preferred unit for analysis. If more highly skilled individuals prefer to work with different classes of unit for translation tasks than less skilled individuals, then we have an interesting additional criterion for assessing performance.

The second coding scheme developed for Gerloff's study sought to identify the different problem-solving strategies used in translation. The protocols collected for this study were analysed at two levels: first, for syntactic attributes of the segments, and second, for the information content of the segments.

Most assessments of performance across a range of linguistic assessment tasks use criteria such as grammatical accuracy, extent of vocabulary, fluency and so on to make judgements about skill. Gerloff's study shows that it is possible that other criteria may be used to make such judgements of skill level.

Dual coding of protocols has been used in other domains. For instance, Green and Gilhooly (1990a) used a hierarchical scheme to examine problem-solving strategies and learning procedures used by novices learning to use a computer. The notion of a hierarchical scheme involves the idea of a macro-unit which subsumes a number of micro-units. Green and Gilhooly used as macro-units general problem-solving episodes and then identified a number of micro-units which were specific to each class of macro-unit. As an example, the general unit 'problem understanding' included smaller units which were coded as instances of understanding behaviour. Macro-units, or episodes, were used in order to examine switches between qualitatively different activities and to identify events that led to a switch from one general episode to another.

Verbal protocol data may be coded in more than one way, using schemes

3 Developing a coding scheme

that are related. Coding data using different schemes differs from assigning a segment of verbal protocol more than one code. The general principle of protocol analysis is that each segment of protocol represents a single process. If more than one code seems to apply to an individual segment, a number of actions is possible:

(i)   The segment may need to be split and coded as two segments.
(ii) The codes in question may be sufficiently similar to merit their fusion to form one coding category.
(iii) The coding scheme may require revisions.

Often, the problem can be solved using either of the first two options above. Occasionally though, the same coding problem occurs and it becomes apparent that the coding scheme has weaknesses and needs to be revised. One cause of the problem is mixing specific with general coding categories. The coding scheme may comprise categories at more than one level of specificity. This then leads to instances where both a general and a more specific category can apply.

To conclude this section then, coding the protocol begins with the identification of what will be the main unit for analysis. It is possible to code segments in more than one way, using complementary schemes. This enables the researcher to gain as much useful information from the protocols as possible.

Points to note:

- A unit for analysis usually corresponds to a phrase, clause or sentence.
- The unit of analysis may vary, depending upon the skill level of the participants in question.
- Hierarchical coding schemes can provide useful information.

Segmenting the protocols

Recall the basic idea, which is that each segment should be representative of a single, specific process. When speaking, individuals do not always speak in grammatical sentences, and a single statement might not always correspond to a sentence – it may be a phrase, or even a word. Segmentation is usually quite straightforward once it becomes clear that a unit for analysis should be a phrase, perhaps just a word or a sentence. Thus, although segmenting a protocol may appear to be quite complex, in practice it can usually be achieved with good reliability.

The previous section introduced the idea of multiple coding. In the case of the Gerloff example, the same segments were simply coded using two different

3 Developing a coding scheme

coding schemes. The Green and Gilhooly example used two quite different classes of segment, and two different coding schemes. The use of broad categories as well as more fine-grained categories can be interesting for considering tasks where activity switches between broad processes.

Consider reading comprehension. A reading comprehension task involves processes of reading, understanding, search, retrieval of information from memory, inferencing and more. The term 'reading' however describes a series of complex cognitive processes. Reading can include simple reading of text, re-reading text and scanning text. All are examples of reading, but each has quite distinct characteristics. Understanding is closely associated with reading in that understanding is about making sense of what has been read. Understanding can involve paraphrasing and drawing of inferences from text. It can be useful to focus on switches between broad categories of processes as well to focus on activity within each category. A switch from an understanding process back to a reading process may signify that a segment of text has not been understood. These sorts of switches can be important because they yield information on the nature of the problem – is there a difficulty with the text that is being used, does the student lack the necessary vocabulary to understand the text, or has understanding failed for some other reason?

Below is an extract from a verbal protocol which has been segmented. The protocol was generated by a student whose task was to write an essay based on a piece of text containing an argument around a topical issue. Segments are delineated with a '/'. Sections of the text which are being read or re-read by the student are shown in italics.

001   Thurston's article seems to start from a premise that advertising is mainly a battle between companies to obtain each other's customers rather than to increase the customer base. /

002   Evidence quoted is that after seeing a car advert we do not rush out to purchase a car. /

003   which is rather a simplistic viewpoint. Or ... /

004   despite all the advertising newspaper sales have not increased in 10 years ... Manufacturers continue to spend ... at the same time advertising ... different brands. /

005   So what is he saying there? /

006   Helped persuade people to ... to switch brands. /
007   Right. No it's not a battle between companies, it's /

3 Developing a coding scheme

008   no we've covered that. Now. Yes. /

009   Countries. Countries such as advertising-free China and Russia have some of the heaviest concentration of smokers in the world. /

010   Smokers in the world. /

011   Now let's just see if we can counter that argument. /

012   No advertising ... anyone aware of the danger? /

013   That would be interesting. Right. /

014   Countries such as advertising-free China and Russia have some of the heaviest concentration of smokers in the world. And countries which have banned advertising, such as Norway, Finland, have seen an increase as advertising in Britain has not prevented the fall in the population of smokers. /

Segmentation of this protocol is quite straightforward. Segment 001 presents the student's interpretation of an argument presented in the text. Segment 002 refers to an argument presented in the text and segment 003 presents an evaluation of that argument. Segment 004 shows the student skimming through the text and then at segment 005, pausing to consider what the main argument is. In segment 006 the student re-reads a part of the text and in segment 007 contradicts his interpretation which was stated in segment 001. In segment 008 the student appears to note that a particular point has been dealt with. Segment 009 shows the student reading and segment 010 shows him focusing on the final clause of the previous section of text. In segment 011, the student sets as a goal finding a counter-argument and in segment 012 considers an aspect of a counter-argument. Segment 013 is a positive evaluation of the proposed counter-argument. Finally, segment 014 shows the student re-reading the previous section of text.

The segments in each case correspond to definable activities. We can distinguish reading, re-reading, evaluation, goal setting and inferencing. Each segment comprises either a sentence, or perhaps two when reading, a phrase or a clause. The example shown above also illustrates very well one characteristic of verbal protocols, which is their apparent lack of fluency and organisation. Just as in spoken language, a verbal protocol is typified by hesitations and false starts, and is not always grammatically correct.

In the example above, a symbol (the '/') has been used to denote a segment boundary, and each segment begins on a new line. In this particular case, the

3 Developing a coding scheme

data were coded using a special set of programs. Automating some of the coding and analysis of verbal protocols is taken up in Chapter 4. It is worth noting again here that data may need to be prepared in special ways to suit coding and analysis using special programs and packages. The decision to use a particular piece of software should therefore be taken at an early stage.

Points to note:

- A segment should correspond to an individual process.
- Data may need to be prepared in special ways to suit the requirements of data analysis programs.

Worked examples

Here we continue with our description of the worked two examples presented in Chapter 2. Each example is broken down to illustrate the stages involved in developing a coding scheme, identifying the unit of analysis and segmenting the protocols.

Example 1

L1 Writing skills

A number of issues were considered in developing a coding scheme for the analysis of the protocols generated by students writing the two different classes of essay. These are discussed in detail below.

Developing a coding scheme

Two schemes were developed to code the protocols generated by students completing the essays. Recall that the two essay tasks had already been examined in order to identify what each task requires of students in order that students might carry out the task. The list of activities in both cases suggests three main phases. The resultant model for Task A is presented in Figure 8.

The model depicted in Figure 8 assumes that in order to perform well on Task A, a student must first define the task appropriately. In phase 2, s/he must read through the information that has been given. The student's representation of the task should govern the assessment of the relevance of the material that is presented. By the end of phase 2, a student should ideally have selected the information that is relevant. S/he might indicate that this has been done by highlighting relevant pieces of text, or by putting to one side those pieces of information that have been judged to be relevant. Having done this, a student enters phase 3. Phase 3 begins with planning. Ideally, a student might allocate some time to deciding how to structure the information that has been judged

3 Developing a coding scheme

Figure 8:
Model of idealised performance for Task A

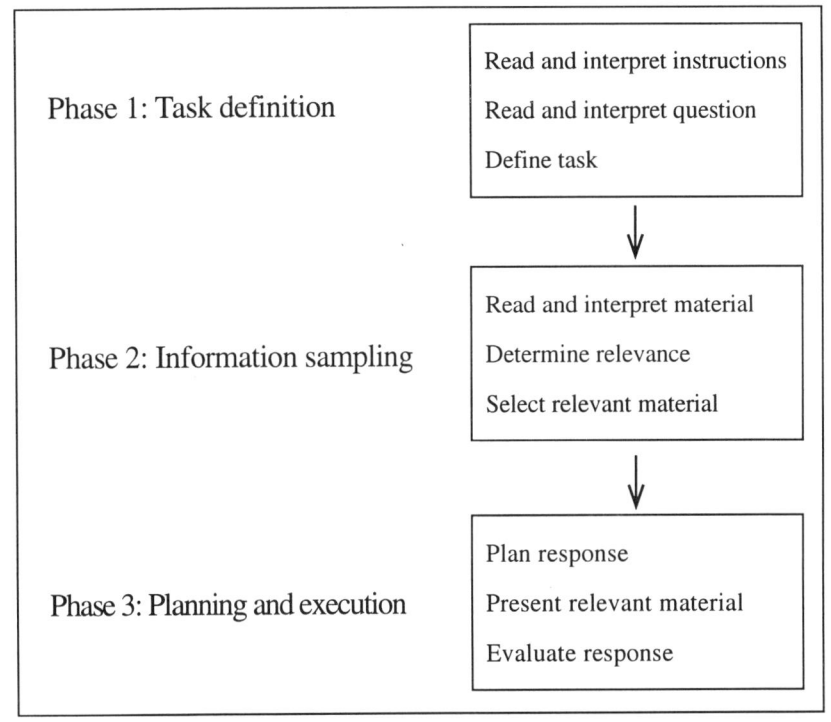

Phase 1: Task definition	Read and interpret instructions Read and interpret question Define task
Phase 2: Information sampling	Read and interpret material Determine relevance Select relevant material
Phase 3: Planning and execution	Plan response Present relevant material Evaluate response

relevant to the response. Once this has been done, the student should begin writing. The task of writing is again influenced by the student's representation of the task. During this phase, if the representation of the task is incomplete or inadequate, the student might refer back to instructions in order to reconstruct or enrich the task representation. Phase 3 should be marked by mon-itoring of progress towards the goal, and by frequent evaluations of work in progress.

Next, we consider the model developed for Task B.

The model of performance illustrated in Figure 9 assumes again that students begin by building a representation of the task. Again, this representation will play a key role in the task of writing the essay. Phase 2 begins with the student reading through the argument that is presented. It is possible that the student might read through the passage more than once. A first pass might be made in order to understand the piece and to identify the main conclusion. During a second pass, the student might engage in cycles of reading the text, and summarising and evaluating the reasoning that is presented.

3 Developing a coding scheme

Figure 9:
Model of idealised performance for Task B

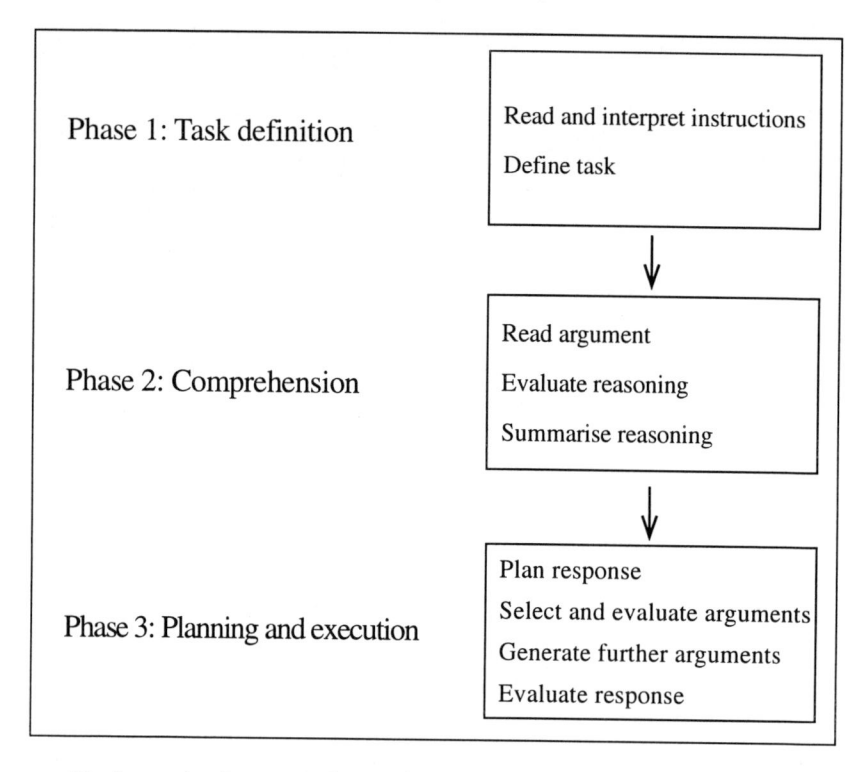

Phase 1: Task definition	Read and interpret instructions Define task

⬇

Phase 2: Comprehension	Read argument Evaluate reasoning Summarise reasoning

⬇

Phase 3: Planning and execution	Plan response Select and evaluate arguments Generate further arguments Evaluate response

Having arrived at an understanding of the structure of the argument, the student may then proceed to plan the essay structure, to select arguments to evaluate and to generate further arguments in response to those presented. During this phase, students are likely to monitor their progress towards the goal, and to evaluate the adequacy of their response.

To a large extent, both models can be extracted by considering the task description and the marking criteria for each essay. We start by looking at Task A.

Task A

The coding scheme was developed by examining a small number of the protocols with the information provided by the task analysis to hand. This preliminary inspection suggested that students appeared to be engaged in a range of quite distinct activities. The main categories, or phases, of behaviour were labelled as follows:

3 Developing a coding scheme

- Task definition
- Information sampling
- Planning and execution

Task definition includes the activities of reading the instructions, reading the question and defining what the task is. Task definition then might culminate with a goal statement, such as, 'Right, so I have to write an essay on ...'.

Information sampling describes the next main phase of activity, during which students should read and interpret the accompanying materials, decide which materials are relevant to the task and then mark or pick out those materials for use when writing.

Finally, during the *planning and execution* phase, students should ideally plan their response to the question, organise their presentation of material determined to be relevant and then evaluate their response to the task.

These three phases then describe the main activities. It is unlikely that students would simply proceed from phase 1 to phase 3 – instead, we should expect to see students switching between the phases.

Within each main category, different category-specific behaviours occurred. For instance, during task definition, students read different things, and read in quite different ways. The task definition category was therefore broken down into sub-categories to denote what was being read (i.e. the instructions or the question). Some students read through the instructions once, others read a little, carried out some interpretation of instructions and then read on.

During an information sampling phase, students might read through all the materials once and then read through a second time. Some students read and then paraphrased whereas other students preferred to skim or scan the text. Some students assessed the relevance of materials and qualified their decision, others did not.

A planning and execution phase was characterised by planning statements, and cycles of writing and evaluation.

The individual codes that were used are presented below, with explanations if the code is not self-explanatory:

Task definition

TD i	Reading instructions
TD ii	Re-reading instructions
TD iii	Interpreting instructions
TD iv	Reading the question
TD v	Re-reading the question
TD vi	Interpreting the question

3 Developing a coding scheme

    TD vii   Goal definition, e.g. 'So I have to do two things here.'

Information sampling
- IS i   Detailed read
- IS ii   Re-reading materials
- IS iii   Focusing, i.e. re-reading something immediately
- IS iv   Paraphrasing materials
- IS v   Skimming or scan reading text
- IS vi   Summarising comment
- IS vii   Mis-reading text
- IS viii   Interpreting text
- IS ix   Misinterpreting text
- IS x   Assessing relevance of information to the task
- IS xi   Assessing some other aspect of information, e.g. 'That's interesting.'
- IS xii   Marking and selecting relevant information for use

Planning and execution
- PE i   Planning structure of essay
- PE ii   Inclusion of marked relevant text
- PE iii   Inclusion of information not already assessed as relevant or other (see above)
- PE iv   Monitoring progress in writing, e.g. 'I'm about halfway through now.'
- PE v   Reading over what has been written
- PE vi   Evaluating what has been written
- PE vii   Evaluating overall response to the task

Finally, two additional codes were used. These were:

Metacomments – these included comments a student might make about how s/he was finding the task. For instance, a student might say, 'I'm having problems thinking about this.'

Miscellaneous – this category was used for any segments that could not be unambiguously coded using one of the codes described above.

Task B

Once again, the coding schemes were developed by first examining a small sample of the protocols. This initial scan of the data again suggested that students engaged in three phases of activity in carrying out the task. The phases were labelled as:

- Task definition.
- Comprehension.
- Planning and execution.

During *task definition,* students attended to instructions, reading these (which included the question to be answered) and interpreting them. Task definition in this case again could culminate in a goal statement.

During a *comprehension* phase, students were likely to read through the presented passage and make sense of the information in a number of different ways. They might also evaluate and summarise the reasoning presented in the argument.

A *planning and execution* phase was again characterised by planning statements, and cycles of writing and evaluation. Selection of relevant arguments and generation of new arguments should also occur here.

The behaviours specific to each phase are outlined below:

Task definition

TD i	Reading instructions
TD ii	Re-reading instructions
TD iii	Interpreting instructions
TD iv	Goal definition

Comprehension

C i	Detailed read
C ii	Re-reading
C iii	Focusing, i.e. re-reading something immediately
C iv	Paraphrasing from the passage
C v	Skimming or scan reading text
C vi	Summarising comment
C vii	Mis-reading text
C viii	Interpreting text
C ix	Misinterpreting text
C x	Evaluating reasoning
C xi	Expressing agreement or disagreement with reasoning presented in text
C xii	Misinterpreting argument
C xiii	Generating a new argument

Planning and execution

PE i	Planning structure of essay
PE ii	Re-stating the presented argument
PE iii	Evaluating the content or topic of an argument
PE iv	Generating a statement or conclusion without supporting reasoning
PE v	Monitoring progress in writing, e.g. 'I'm about halfway through now.'
PE vi	Reading over what has been written
PE vii	Evaluating what has been written
PE viii	Evaluating overall response to the task

Again, two additional codes were used. These were:

Metacomments – these again included comments a student might make about how s/he was finding the task. For instance, a student might say, 'I'm having problems thinking about this.'

Miscellaneous – this category was used for any segments that could not be unambiguously coded using one of the codes described above.

The coding schemes were developed after a number of readings of the sample protocols, and both coding schemes were revised in the light of discussions. Neither coding scheme is used here to make any claims about a particular theory or about specific cognitive processes in writing. Rather, the schemes are used to illustrate an approach for coding protocol data.

Identifying the main unit for analysis

We noted earlier that a unit for analysis will usually be a phrase, clause or sentence and each segment will represent a different process. The coding scheme specifies what these different processes are. For instance, reading the question is one process. Segmentation proceeded by delineating sections of protocol that were defined by pauses or by syntactic breaks. Since the students in this particular study were asked to read some text and write an essay based on that text, a unit for analysis also included sequences of sentences. This is because reading a series of sentences without pause for inference or interpretation engages just one process. If the reading is interspersed with additional verbalisations, then it is more likely that an individual sentence or phrase will comprise the basic unit. In this example then, the unit for analysis was quite easily identified.

3 Developing a coding scheme

Segmenting the protocols

The example below shows how one particular section of protocol was segmented. Each segment in the example corresponds to a distinct process. Once again, a '/ ' is used to denote a segment boundary.

001   The question is: 'The editor of your local newspaper has asked you for an article which would give readers an account of the work of the Citizens' Advice Bureau. Using the material provided, write such an article showing the sort of work these advisers do and why a service such as this is so important.' /

002   Right, so I'm going to have a look at the information here that's given, and, which seems to be all about the Citizens' Advice Bureau. /

003   What's the question? 'Give readers an account of the work', /

004   right, it's two parts, you have to talk about the work and also why it's important. /

The set of protocols were segmented just as shown above. The protocols were then ready for coding. In this case, the segment markers played a special role in that data were entered into a software package for coding. A segment was identified by its segment marker. The coder was given the option of coding segments in sequence, or randomly. The package was developed by Gilhooly and C. Green (1989) and supported the coding and analysis of verbal protocol data. The coding and analysis of these data are described in detail in Chapter 4.

Example 2

Marker strategies in assessing CAE compositions

In this section we go on to describe what was involved in developing a coding scheme, determining the unit for analysis and segmenting the protocols for the marker strategies study.

Developing a coding scheme

The marker strategies project extended the study carried out by Milanovic *et al.* (1992). In Chapter 2, we noted that the 1992 study identified four different strategies used by examiners when marking CPE and FCE compositions. To recap, these were:

- Principled two scan/read – read twice before deciding on a final mark.

- Pragmatic two scan/read – read twice for a specific purpose before

3 Developing a coding scheme

deciding on a final mark.
- Read through – read once and decide on a final mark once the script has been read.
- Provisional mark – make an initial assessment while reading and continue reading to confirm or alter the initial assessment.

The earlier study then provided a starting point for the development of a coding scheme for a larger set of data. One aim was to devise a coding scheme that allowed the researchers to test the hypothesis that these strategies might generalise to the marking of CAE compositions.

A sample of the protocols were selected and examined. This provided a general overview of examiner behaviour and allowed the researchers to identify the different factors noted by examiners as the scripts were marked. Some marking categories were suggested by the marking criteria that examiners are requested to use.

Three main categories of behaviour emerged from this preliminary inspection of the subset of protocols. These were:

Marking behaviour

This main category describes what examiners did while marking and includes four main groups of activities. Within each main group are a number of different activities. The groups and the subsidiary activities are:

A1 Initial reaction to the script

A1i   overview
             This is laid out well

A2 Reading

A2i   detailed read
             Let's start reading then, Yesterday I went to see ...
A2ii   summarising comment
             This person's got the essential points
A2iii   skimming/scanning for a specific purpose
             Just scanning through it again now
A2iv   reference to question paper
             I'm just going back to the question here for a minute
A2v   comparison of sections of the script/other scripts
             Not as good as some of the previous ones I've seen

3 Developing a coding scheme

A3 Mark

A3i   1st indication of mark
OK, this looks like a 5 already.

A3ii   review/discussion of mark/re-assessment
4 or 5? Some things are 5, other things are 4.

A3iii   reference to mark scheme
4 does say 'errors only when more complex language attempted'

A3iv   confirmation of mark
Yes, definitely a 4.

A3v   mark decision
Again, I think, I would give her 5 for that.

A4 Personal response

A4i   age of candidate
Perhaps a mature student?

A4ii   nationality of candidate
French I suppose. Toulouse.

A4iii   reference to own teaching
That's not the way I would have taught that

A4iv   reference to other marking experience
Probably not even a particularly good first certificate level

A4v   marker's attitude
I'm getting negative feelings about this one

A4vi   assumption about candidate's knowledge
Yeah, so there's obviously been some learning of idioms and more colloquial language

A4vii   marker's inference
I think that's an attempt at a joke

B1 Arrangements of meaning

B1i   genre convention/format
but no salutation or 'yours sincerely'

B1ii   coherence/clarity/convincing writing
It's a bit unclear here

B1iii   organisation, ordering of ideas/conciseness/control
It's not so well organised

3 Developing a coding scheme

B2 Appropriate language

B2i	register: appropriateness of language	
	Well, that's the wrong register	
B2ii	grammar/phraseology	
	That's an unusual sort of phrase	
B2iii	vocabulary: sophistication, appropriateness	
	rather odd use of the word 'claim'	
B2iv	expression/style/flow/fluency/range/originality	
	Well it's pretty well expressed actually	
B2v	influence of mother tongue	
	French mistake here	

B3 Technical features

B3i	vocabulary: accuracy of meaning	
	Well, not quite the right word but we know what she means	
B3ii	spelling (accuracy)	
	nevertheless 'netherless'	
B3iii	grammar (accuracy)	
	... , the tenses are all over the place	
B3iv	punctuation (accuracy)	
	It's got nice use of inverted commas	
B3v	legibility/neatness/handwriting	
	horrible writing	
B3vi	setting out of paragraphs/layout	
	well laid out	
B3vii	general linguistic accuracy	
	the language is good	
B3viii	cohesion	
	there's no cohesion	

B4 Task realisation

B4i	length	
	Perhaps a little long	
B4ii	response to global understanding of task	
	I really don't think it's answering the question	
B4iii	lifting from the question sheet	
	well that's lifted from the rubric	
B4iv	points covered/relevance/content	
	I don't think all the points in the rubric are covered	
B4v	effect on target reader	
	I think the target reader would be confused	
B4vi	completion of all of the task	
	completed the task	

B4vii   accuracy of understanding the letter and newspaper report quoted within the question paper
so they've misunderstood the actual situation here

Evaluative responses

The second main category centres on the evaluative responses made by examiners as the scripts are read and marked. Evaluative responses were coded as positive, negative or neutral.

Evaluative response of the marker
3   positive response
2   neutral response
1   negative response
0   query

Metacomments

Finally, the third category of response includes metacomments, such as comments made by examiners on their own marking technique, and miscellaneous comments that could not be coded using the other existing codes, e.g, *'I'm having some problems deciding what to do here.'*

These coding categories do not individually represent any of the four main strategies that were identified in the 1992 study. A strategy does not correspond to a single process however, and so it would make little sense to devise a coding scheme that focused entirely on the level of gross strategies. A strategy may be inferred from the overall pattern of activity shown.

Identifying the main unit for analysis

Once again, a unit for analysis was considered to be a clause, phrase, sentence or group of sentences. The latter again can make for quite large segments, but this is a consequence of the task used – marking scripts requires examiners to first read those scripts, and some examiners may engage the read process for a relatively large proportion of time before engaging another process.

Segmenting the protocols

Data from the study were next segmented and prepared for coding.

An example of a segmented protocol is presented below. Again, a '/ ' is used to delineate each segment, the segments have been numbered and each segment begins on a new line.

001   Beginning with the note to Malcolm. Dear Malcolm, Thank you for your last letter. I am really sorry that this paper got everything wrong and that you have got to bear the consequences. I hope people still

3 Developing a coding scheme

talk to you. Please find enclosed a copy of the letter for which you were asking. I hope it meets your expectations. I did not put too much emphasis on all facts which are wrong but I tried to stress that you have not been the mugger. /

002   Not too bad this note. /

003   Dear Sirs, Your article 'Handbag Thief Caught' from Wednesday May 27 1992. I address to you referring to your paper's article mentioned above. As I read it I was quite astonished and I would like to draw your attention to some misunderstandings which occur in this article. You give the impression that it was Mr Malcolm Taylor who attempted to steal the woman's handbag. This is completely wrong. It was me, a German, not an American who accompanied Mr Taylor at the evening in question. Therefore please allow me to state shortly what has really happened. Mr Taylor and I were on our way home from the cinema as we saw a young man who attempted to snatch the handbag of a woman passing by. It was me who tried to help the woman. As a result I suffered a cut to my face. Fortunately Miss Erskine has not been injured in this incident but unfortunately the thief managed to escape. Please note that Mr Taylor has not been directly involved. As Mr Taylor's reputation suffered from your incorrect report I want to kindly ask you to publish this letter to put things right. I may allow me to thank you in advance. I hope I could help you in this matter. Write soon. /

004   He says this is completely wrong, so is this! /

005   He says he suffered the cuts, that's novel, /

006   the tenses are all over the place and it's a bit heavy. /

007   Malcolm's letter is better, the letter to Malcolm is better than the one to the editor. I quite like some of it, /

008   'I was quite astonished', I quite like that but he gives the impression that he was the thief. /

009   'You give the impression that it was Mr Malcolm Taylor who attempted to steal the woman's handbag. This is completely wrong. It was me ...' /

010   I had to go on and on reading, he hasn't really done the task that he

3 Developing a coding scheme

should. /

011   I would give him 2. /

The segmentation was carried out using a standard word processing package. Each identified segment was presented on a new line. This breaks up the entire protocol into easily identifiable visual units, and makes the task of coding much easier.

Summary

This chapter has discussed in detail the issues central to the segmenting and coding of verbal protocol data. The development of an appropriate coding scheme can be a particularly difficult task. The worked examples illustrate just how hard it can be to capture adequately the contents of a verbal report in a form that lends itself to subsequent analysis. Detail may have to be sacrificed in order to maintain adequate levels of reliability.

Tutorial exercise

Appendix IV contains protocols generated by students working on a cloze passage. The procedure adopted is slightly unusual because the students worked in pairs on each passage. The protocols indicate which student is speaking at any given point. All four students are English native speakers working on a cloze passage in English, their first language.

Your task is to do the following:

(i)   Develop a coding scheme for analysing these protocols.
(ii)   Identify what the unit for analysis will be.
(iii)   Segment the protocols.

Bear in mind that although the protocols were generated by students working in pairs, we can still develop a coding scheme centred on information that students were attending to as they worked on the task.

In order to carry out this task, you will need to refer to the following materials:

(i) The questions that were attempted by the students.
(ii) The instructions that were given to the students.

Appendix IV provides some guidance on how to approach this task.

4 Analysing verbal protocol data

Introduction

This chapter concentrates on techniques for coding and analysing verbal protocol data. Once again, there is a tutorial exercise at the end of the chapter to enable the reader to try out some of the techniques learned here.

Coding the protocols

Once the protocols have been segmented, coding begins. There are two related goals in coding.

One goal is to assign a code unambiguously to each identified segment of protocol. In the previous chapter, we discussed the idea of developing a coding scheme on one part of the protocol data and then testing it on the rest.

A second goal is to encode the data as objectively as possible. A naive encoder may hold or be exposed to biases which can influence the way in which the protocol is encoded. Ambiguity in the statements that comprise the verbal protocol allows these biases to manifest themselves. However, context can play a role in disambiguating a protocol. Take an example of a reading comprehension task. A student thinking aloud might say, 'There was something about this in question 1.' There is clearly insufficient information within the segment itself to understand precisely what the student is referring to. We can try to identify the subject of this segment by using task relevant information. For instance, if question 1 and the current question have one subject in common then the ambiguous segment may be coded as a reference to that particular subject. If the questions have more than one topic in common, however, it may not be possible to disambiguate the segment. Disambiguating a protocol can be a complex task. Quite often, sections of protocol cannot reliably be assigned any code. If there is uncertainty about the content of the segment in question, this can be noted by using a 'miscellaneous' coding category, and by not entering segments coded in this way into the final analysis.

Establishing the reliability of codings

A coding scheme should be understandable and usable by individuals other than the developer of the scheme. Quite apart from issues of validity and reliability, coding schemes that are readily understood and usable are easily portable.

One of the first steps to be carried out once data have been coded is to establish the reliability of codings to ensure that coding does not reflect the biases or idiosyncrasies of one individual. This is particularly important since the validity of any inferences and conclusions that may be drawn from the analysis of the coded data depends on achieving a satisfactory level of encoder reliability.

It is helpful to distinguish between two different methods of establishing encoder reliability.

Inter-coder reliability

Inter-coder reliability refers to the level of agreement between two independent coders coding the same verbal protocols. Inter-coder reliability may be established in a number of ways. The method chosen may depend on resources available, size of the dataset and skill of the chosen coders.

Where only a small number of verbal reports have been gathered, it may be feasible to ensure that all reports are coded by both coders. A direct comparison of codings then allows reliability to be estimated in a very straightforward manner. The estimate of reliability may be calculated as the proportion of segments where codes have been agreed divided by the total number of segments.

In practice, it is not always possible to use two independent coders. If this is the case then other methods are used to check the consistency of codings. One alternative is to recruit a second coder to code a subset of those segments already coded by the first coder. This provides a measure of how usable the coding scheme is, and can highlight problems in the use of particular coding categories. The level of agreement in the subject of segments also gives a clear indication of inter-coder reliability.

Intra-coder reliability

A different approach involves one coder coding all segments twice. This provides a measure of intra-coder reliability. Intra-coder reliability examines consistency within an individual's codings, but makes assumptions that may not be upheld. It is not the most desirable method for two main reasons. The first is that any given coder may consistently make the same sorts of coding errors, and double coding might not reveal this. The second is that coders may remember the codes they have used to code particular segments of the verbal report. Despite these reservations, intra-coder reliability can still be established in the same way as inter-coder reliability.

Expressing encoder reliability

Reliability can be expressed as the percentage agreement between coders as

4 *Analysing verbal protocol data*

suggested above, but such a simple measure of reliability is not ideal. In practice, some coding categories occur more frequently than others. A straightforward calculation of overall agreement then will largely reflect the degree of agreement where the most frequent categories are concerned. If, for instance, 45% of the total codings reflect the use of just two categories, and if raters disagree (or agree) more on the use of these two categories than they do on the use of another two categories that occur much less frequently, then overall estimates of reliability will be deflated (or inflated). A more robust measure of reliability assesses the extent of agreement between coders for each individual code. In practice, it is best to maintain as high levels of reliability as possible, even at the expense of reducing the level of detail of the coding scheme.

Summary

Assessing encoder reliability is an important phase in protocol analysis. It is preferable to have a second independent coder code at least a proportion of the segments that are to be coded by the principal coder. When this is not possible, efforts should be made to have at least a subset of the protocols coded twice by one or ideally two individuals.

Points to note:

- Encoder reliability must be assessed when verbal protocols are used.
- Inter-coder reliability is a measure of agreement between individuals.
- Intra-coder reliability is a measure of one individual's consistency.
- Reliability is usually expressed as a percentage.

Data analysis techniques

In earlier chapters we noted that various software packages now exist for the purpose of coding and analysing qualitative data, and more specifically, verbal protocol data. In this section we discuss some of the most useful and frequently used data analysis techniques and we describe some of the software that has been developed.

Analysing qualitative data is time consuming, and it is not a task that may feasibly be attempted by hand, unless the data set is extremely small. Most researchers make use of a range of specialised techniques in addition to statistical analysis.

Techniques

The sorts of analyses that will be carried out will depend largely on the aims of the study. Studies using verbal protocol analysis often make extensive use of just a few basic approaches:

(i) Contrasting group designs.
(ii) Profiling.
(iii) Errors analysis.

Contrasting group studies usually seek to identify commonalities within groups of individuals, and factors differentiating those groups. Profiling studies are often used to construct profiles of individuals, in order to describe individual behaviour. Errors analysis is sometimes seen as a distinct approach since the focus for the analysis takes errors data rather than solution latencies or overall scores. The analysis of errors data is very relevant to research on educational instruction and assessment. None of these three broad approaches is mutually exclusive.

Contrasting group designs

Consider the case where a small group ($N = 20$) of students is asked to take a new test in order to assess their skills in translating French (L2) to English (L1). The test scores range from 85% down to a low 20%. Scores on the test correlate highly with the same students' scores on a standard test of translation skill. Thus, the test developers are reasonably confident that their new test measures translation skill, and that it discriminates well. However, performance on both tests reveals little about the nature of translation skill – it does not inform the researchers about what it is that good translators have acquired, or whether poorer translators are using similar but less well-developed skills, or using rather different approaches entirely. If the skill changes as it develops, are different things measured by the test at different stages of skill development?

One way to address some of these questions is to use verbal protocols in addition to collecting performance data. Thus, continuing with the example above, performance data (or other quantitative data) might be used to identify groups within the main group of candidates. Score ranges (e.g. 0% – 10%, 11% – 20%, 21% – 30% and so on), grades (e.g. A, B, C, D, and E) or some other criteria (e.g. 'fail', 'average', 'pass', 'distinction') might be used. Whichever criteria are used, the purpose of the exercise is to find some independent means by which to subdivide the main group into performance-related groups. Supposing candidates in this case are divided into five main groups on the basis of their grades, where possible grades are A, B, C, D and E. We might expect different numbers of students within each group, the bulk of students achieving an average C grade, and fewer students achieving the very

4 Analysing verbal protocol data

high and the very low grades. Once differentiated into groups, we can then begin to examine the verbal protocol data.

Assuming that a coding scheme has been developed, we could begin the task of analysing the data in a straightforward fashion by calculating code frequencies and code-code transition frequencies (the frequency with which one particular behaviour was followed by another particular behaviour). The specific statistical tests that might be used in order to examine differences between groups depend on factors such as sample size, number of different codes and so on. T-tests, analysis of variance and discriminant analysis are all potential statistical tests that might be applied in order to examine differences between groups. Other tests may be used in order to examine whether there is evidence of an association between a given behaviour and a particular measure of performance. For instance, chi-square is suitable if candidates each contribute one observation. An example is presented below to give an indication of the application of a statistical technique, and to show how results may be interpreted.

Example

Some think aloud protocols were gathered from a group of twenty students, each working on a multiple choice test of reading. The students each answered five questions. The researchers were interested in the difficulty level of the passage, and strategies students use to select a response.

A '*' denotes the correct response in each case.

Question	Number of students selecting each of the options				
	I	II	III	IV	V
1	5	7*	2	4	2
2	8*	3	3	4	2
3	1	2	10*	3	4
4	2	1	1	14*	2
5	4	3	5	1	7*

Questions 1, 2 and 5 were more difficult than questions 3 and 4. Analysis of the protocols indicated that a source of difficulty was complexity of reasoning presented in sections of the text that pertained to these three questions.

The researchers then went on to examine the protocols produced by the students. Five main strategies were identified, and these are labelled A, B, C, D and E. Students thus appeared to use one of these strategies in answering a given question.

A chi-square analysis was used to determine whether there was any association between strategy used and correct responses. The data are shown below:

Strategy	Question				
	1	2	3	4	5
A	5	4	7	8	3
B	1	2	0	3	1
C	0	1	1	2	1
D	0	1	2	0	2
E	1	0	1	1	0

The analysis showed that there was a strong association between strategy use and obtaining a correct response. The strength of the association derives from a link between use of strategy A and correct responding.

This brief example illustrates ways in which verbal protocols might be used to address questions that arise during test development and evaluation.

Profiling

Profiling is suited to situations where a picture of an individual or group of individuals performing at particular levels is required. For instance, if we wished to construct a picture of an exceptionally good translator, we might go about the task by profiling the skills of just a few highly skilled translators. No assumptions need be made about homogeneity of skill, since individual profiles may be constructed and compared.

Profile construction using verbal protocols makes extensive use of code frequency data and code-code transition frequency data. For instance, let us assume that students adopt different strategies when asked to compose a short piece as part of a test of L2 writing skills. The task analysis and review of relevant literature might suggest that students may adopt any one of perhaps five different strategies. Relevant questions might be:

(i)   Is there any association between the strategy used and performance?
(ii) Do students consistently use the same strategy (or strategies)?
(iii) If students switch strategy, what triggers the switch?

To address such questions, we need to construct a picture of sequences of heeded information. These may then be compared with sequences that might be predicted by different models of the composing process.

A protocol generated by a student working on even a short composition task can be lengthy. The procedure for analysing a set of such protocols can be simplified. One method is to divide the protocols into chunks, each chunk representing a distinct phase of activity, e.g. a 'reading' phase, a 'planning' phase, a 'writing' phase and so on. If the protocols are quite brief, they may be best dealt with in their entirety. To construct a profile, code-code transition data need to be carefully examined. These data embody the sequences of heeded information. Consider the example below, which shows an initial behaviour (the 'code') and the behaviour that immediately followed it (the 'consequent') for two hypothetical students:

Table 2:
Example code-code transition frequencies

Code	Consequent	Student 1 (%)	Student 2 (%)
read	re-read	25	60
read	paraphrase	70	20
read	scan	5	20

Student 1 generally reads and then paraphrases, whereas Student 2 does not show quite such a clear pattern, although there is a high incidence of re-reading. In the case of both students, re-reading seems to be triggered by a comprehension failure. Paraphrasing, which indicates understanding, occurs much more frequently in the case of Student 1 than Student 2. Having noted these general patterns, we might wish to go on to explore reasons for comprehension failure. For instance, is it specific to the task in question, or does it suggest a general skill deficiency?

Frequency data of this kind can be used effectively to construct visual profiles of behaviour for the task in question. These profiles or representations may take the form of 'transition nets' similar to those referred to by Ericsson and Simon (1993), or may take alternative forms. The general approach of conceptual maps for instance may be adopted in order to represent the content of verbalisations and to capture any verbalised links between heeded information. Conceptual maps display in visual form concepts, or ideas, and any links between these ideas. Links may be represented implicitly by proximity of concepts to one another, or more explicitly by labelling the link. The links are specific to the individual, and different individuals may represent and organise knowledge in different ways. The idea that knowledge is structured is not a new one – researchers have used the umbrella of schema theory for some time in order to explore knowledge structures. Other more quantitative techniques that may be used to examine the organisation of information include the use of multidimensional scaling techniques, and linked or weighted networks such as Pathfinder, developed by Roger Schvaneveldt and discussed in Schvaneveldt *et al.* (1985).

If the task at hand were one of mental addition, answering research questions like those above might be simpler – mental addition tasks tend to be brief, strategies can be quite readily identified and the outcome, or answer, may be objectively evaluated. Writing a short composition in L2 is an extended activity, and so it is unlikely that actual behaviour will exactly match that predicted by any given model. Nevertheless, different patterns may be discernible between and even within students. One problem for the researcher is in deciding how closely different patterns should match before the researcher may conclude that the same or different strategies are being used. Strategies may be task dependent, or it may be that particular aspects of a task incite some students to deviate from their usual pattern of behaviour, but not other students.

We should note one final point about the construction of profiles and the empirical evaluation of predictions. Where tasks are formal and well specified, such as mathematical reasoning tasks, individuals may show quite regular sequences of processing. This allows the researcher to make strong predictions, not just about the nature of the heeded information, but also its sequence. Most tasks in the domain of language testing are less well defined and may be considered informal. It is therefore less likely that such strong predictions may be made. Instead, predictions may be restricted to a specification of a set of states of heeded information and more general patterns of behaviour, rather than to identifying precise sequences of heeded information and cognitive processes.

Errors analysis

Finally, we consider the analysis of errors. Errors are often discarded in favour of the use of correct or accurate responses to questions and tasks. Analysing errors is extremely informative though, providing information on knowledge deficits, as well as inefficient or 'buggy' strategies, and also serving to identify questions or tasks that are themselves flawed. Errors need not always be seen as evidence of the shortcomings of the individual – they often tell us about poor question and task design.

Verbal protocols reveal the errors that individuals make as a task is being carried out. These errors may go unchecked and remain in the final response to the task, or they may be identified and corrected when detected. Detection may occur as soon as the error is made, shortly afterwards, or much later during checking.

A distinction is frequently made between types of errors (e.g. Norman 1981, 1988; Reason 1979). Norman describes his distinction between slips and mistakes. Slip errors occur when an act is not carried out as intended. These include speech errors (such as spoonerisms), starting an act and then forgetting what the original intention was, and a range of seemingly random

4 Analysing verbal protocol data

errors that appear to occur when the human information processing system is overloaded. Mistakes are generally held to be knowledge-based in that mistakes are made because requisite knowledge is either missing or faulty. The role of intentionality captures the distinction well, since slips are often recognised by the perpetrator to be errors, whereas mistakes are not.

Verbal protocols shed light on the nature of the errors and can provide explanations for their occurrence. This can be especially important in the development of new assessment instruments and in pretesting materials. Assessment instruments can be prone to guessing, and a correct guess is not always distinguishable from a correct response. 'False negatives' (responses that are wrong, but not as a result of the candidate's knowledge or skill) are just as important to identify as the 'false positives' (correct guesses). Both hint at problems with the instrument itself. Verbal protocols may be used to ensure that correct and incorrect answers are achieved for legitimate reasons.

Individuals learning a new language make a range of errors on different assessment tasks. It can be informative to attempt a taxonomy of different error types for a given task, and to identify as far as possible what gives rise to the different errors. For instance, one might anticipate that individuals differing in skill level would vary not just in the number of errors made, but also in the nature of those errors.

Quantitative data on errors, such as overall frequency and the incidence of different types of errors, may be analysed using appropriate statistical tests. Qualitative data on errors that are revealed through the analysis of verbal protocols require a different approach. A useful first step that might be considered is to attempt to distinguish between slips, or unintentional errors, and mistakes. This would serve to highlight those errors that may be due to deficiencies in the knowledge base.

In practice, it is much more difficult to achieve this and the conceptual distinction between slips and mistakes does not hold up as well as it might (Payne and Squibb 1990). Nevertheless, some progress may be made by focusing on knowledge-based errors, since these should occur consistently. They may be indicated in protocols by hesitation, or statements suggesting uncertainty about the chosen action (e.g. over the correct spelling of a word, or an appropriate German verb meaning 'to type').

Software

A small number of packages and programs have been developed to automate to differing degrees the coding and analysis of verbal data. Some of these are described below, to illustrate the range of functions that are useful in coding and analysing verbal protocol data.

4 Analysing verbal protocol data

Gilhooly and Green's suite of programs for protocol analysis

The suite of programs developed in SNOBOL and SPITBOL by Gilhooly and C. Green (1989) offered the researcher support in coding verbal protocols and in carrying out some basic analyses. While the programs themselves have been superseded, many of the ideas upon which the programs were based remain highly relevant. In fact, the list of features described below might usefully serve as a checklist for a researcher interested in automating the coding and analysis of protocols.

The suite of programs offered, amongst other things, routines for:
(i) Coding segments of protocol.
(ii) Random and sequential presentation of segments for coding.
(iii) Optional viewing of context, i.e. the immediately preceding and immediately following segments of protocol.
(iv) Changing a code after the original coding.
(v) Collapsing codes.
(vi) Counting the frequency with which each code was used by any given coder.
(vii) Computing inter-coder or intra-coder reliability.
(viii) Counting the frequency of particular words within a protocol, the total words in a protocol, and the total time taken to carry out the task in question.
(ix) Calculating statistics for word frequency and solution latency data.
(x) Computing code-code transition frequencies.

These sorts of routines can be readily developed using today's modern systems, notably UNIX systems with their powerful string processing capabilities. Usually, if data are stored in text format and if segments are indic-ated using an identifiable character, manipulations may be carried out. Most modern word processing packages include conversion programs that allow data to be converted into formats suitable for use with other packages, such as statistical and spreadsheet packages.

NUDIST (Non-numerical Unstructured Data Indexing, Searching and Theorising)

NUDIST[3] is a commercially available package used for structuring and indexing qualitative data. Although not specifically designed for analysing verbal protocol data, it can be used for preliminary analyses and for preparing data for further coding and analysis.

---

3 NUDIST was developed by Tom and Lyn Richards at La Trobe University, Victoria, Australia.

4 *Analysing verbal protocol data*

Data, which may be in the form of verbal protocols, interview transcripts, questionnaire responses and so on, are entered using the package. Documents may be divided into text units, and entered using the package. Text units are the basic units upon which NUDIST operates. For the purposes of protocol analysis then, a text unit corresponds to a segment. NUDIST allows the researcher to browse through text in different ways, to search for particular words or phrases for instance. Hierarchical index systems may be created, and this facility can be helpful if hierarchical coding schemes are being considered or used.

The range of functions NUDIST offers includes:
i)   Text retrieval and coding.
ii) Retrieval of stored relations between indexing categories.
iii) Constructing new categories from already existing categories.
iv) Document browsing.

The hierarchical indexing facility allows trees of categories and subcategories to be constructed. Furthermore, data may be structured in more than one way, so that the same piece of information might be listed under more than one heading. Once data are indexed, operations may be carried out on both the tree structure that is created and the data represented by 'nodes' contained within the tree.

Other approaches

Ericsson and Simon (1993) describe some research which aimed to semi-automate the analysis of verbal protocols. The program, SAPA (semi-automatic protocol analysis) was developed by Bhaskar and Simon (1977). SAPA sought to capture protocol contents by predicting the order in which operations would be applied by human solvers. The SAPA program incorporated some basic knowledge about the problem-solving strategies that might be applied in the domain of thermodynamics. This basic knowledge enabled it to generate predictions about probable operations that could then be verified by a human coder. Applications such as these require a well developed understanding of the domain in question.

In everyday situations, the domains in which tasks are carried out and the problems with which individuals are faced are less well defined. Thus, the development of coding schemes and the preliminary coding of verbal protocols tends to be carried out manually.

Points to note:

- Verbal protocols, once coded, may be analysed using a range of

commonly used statistical tests.
- The coding and analysis of verbal protocols may be automated to varying degrees with the assistance of special software packages and special programs.

Worked examples

Next, we continue our breakdown and analysis of the two worked examples. In the following sections we discuss the coding of the protocols, issues in establishing the reliability of the codings, and some of the different ways in which the data were analysed. In both cases, very detailed analyses of data were carried out. Rather than present both analyses in their entirety, we shall present contrasting aspects of the data analysis.

Example 1

Writing skills

Having described the broad approaches students are assumed to take in order to perform well on the tasks, the next step was to analyse the think aloud protocols in order to determine what students actually did. Our discussion focuses on some of the quantitative analyses that were carried out.

Coding the protocols

We begin by looking at some predictions that were made about anticipated performance of students who were likely to do well on each of the two tasks. The predictions were derived from an overview of relevant research on writing skills, and from the task analysis.

Task A: Good students should show more evidence of determining the relevance of information, planning and evaluation. Poor students should show less evidence of these activities, and might show more evidence of other activities, such as misinterpretation, spurious selection of material, and erroneous judgements of the relevance of material.

Task B: It was anticipated that good students should show evidence of critical evaluation and the generation of further arguments. Poor students might fail to evaluate critically, or might make evaluation errors, and should show less evidence of presenting further arguments. Good students might show more evidence of processing associated with the use of the knowledge-transforming rather than the knowledge-telling strategy. Poor students on the other hand might be expected to show more evidence of knowledge-telling than knowledge-transforming.

The coding of protocols commenced thus. Each segment of protocol, representing a statement made by a student, was assigned one code. Ambiguous segments that could not be disambiguated were coded as 'miscellaneous'.

4 Analysing verbal protocol data

The coding of the protocols was carried out within a popular word processing package. Files comprising the codes allocated to each numbered segment were constructed. Data contained within these files were then analysed. This is described below.

Establishing encoder reliability

The entire set of protocols were coded by one researcher. A second researcher coded 20% of the set of protocols. Agreement between coders was established to be over 85%. A reliability estimate was not calculated for each individual code since there was no evidence that a small number of codes accounted for the majority of coded instances of behaviour.

Data analysis

We analysed the verbal protocols in a systematic way. First, files containing coded data were divided into two equal groups (four good scripts and four poor scripts) for each task on the basis of marks awarded by one independent examiner. The first analyses addressed two questions:

i) Was there any evidence of differences in number of segments between groups?
ii) Was there any evidence that groups vary in number of different behaviours?

Question 1 was essentially concerned with the frequency with which individuals switched from one behaviour to another. One way to establish the extent to which subjects switched from one behaviour to another is to focus on the number of segments within the protocols. Frequent switching between behaviours will give rise to a greater number of segments. Question 2 was concerned with the range of different behaviours elicited by the two tasks, and whether this range varied for good and poor scripts. The data are presented in Tables 3 and 4 below.

Table 3:

Average number of segments per good and poor script for each essay type

	Task B	Task A
Good scripts	57.33	73.3
Poor scripts	38.2	53.7

4 Analysing verbal protocol data

Table 3 shows that, irrespective of writing task, good students switched between behaviours more frequently than did poorer students.

Table 4:

Average number of different behaviours per good and poor script for each essay type

	Task B	Task A
Good scripts	23.67	30.3
Poor scripts	15	25

Table 4 goes further and shows that good students exhibited a wider range of different behaviours than poorer students. Thus, a brief analysis of quantitative aspects of the verbal protocols revealed some interesting differences between able and less able students. There were also task effects. Task A evoked a greater frequency of behavioural switches and a wider range of different behaviours than did Task B. This is unlikely to be an artefact of differences in coding schemes, since the two schemes included a similar number of different behavioural categories (28 in the case of Task A and 27 in the case of Task B).

Next, we consider the question of the relationship, if any, between the two tasks. One simple way to address this question is to focus on performance data and to calculate the correlation between performance on the two tasks. Students had been ranked according to their position in the group. Thus, '1st' indicates that the student produced the best essay in the group, and '8th' indicates that the student produced the worst essay in the group. Rankings of students are shown below in Table 5.

Table 5:

Rankings of students on Task A and on Task B

Student	Task A	Task B
A	1st	1st
B	2nd	6th
C	3rd	4th
D	4th	3rd
E	5th	5th
F	6th	2nd
G	7th	7th
H	8th	8th

4 Analysing verbal protocol data

With the exception of students B and F, most students achieved the same relative group position on both tasks. Thus, performance on the two tasks correlated quite strongly. We cannot infer a great deal though from these preliminary analyses about quantitative differences between the tasks. In order to learn more, we need to examine the verbal protocols in detail. We turn next to the analysis of the verbal protocol data.

Frequency data were obtained first in order to determine the patterns of cognitive activity associated with carrying out the two different writing tasks. The main findings are summarised below. Alongside each behavioural category are two columns, the first presenting frequency data for good students, the second presenting frequency data for poor students. The frequency data represent the mean frequency with which each behaviour occurred for good and poor students. A '*' is used to denote instances where good and poor students differed significantly in the frequency with which they engaged in the behaviour in question.

Task A

Recall that Task A comprised three broad phases of activity. These were:

- Task definition
- Information sampling
- Planning and execution

Frequency data (mean)

Task definition	*Good students*	*Poor students*
TD i Reading instructions	1.2	1.1
TD ii Re-reading instructions	0.6	1.4
TD iii Interpreting instructions	2.3	0.9*
TD iv Reading the question	1.5	1.7
TD v Re-reading the question	0.4	1.8*
TD vi Interpreting the question	1.1	0.6
TD vii Goal definition	2.4	0.6*

During the goal definition stage, we find differences between the two groups of students on three behaviours. Good students more frequently interpret instructions and set goals than do poorer students. Poor students more frequently re-read the question. It is probable that re-reading the question occurs because the task is insufficiently defined by poor students.

Information sampling		Good students	Poor students
IS i	Detailed read	8.1	4.4*
IS ii	Re-reading materials	3.6	5.5*
IS iii	Focusing	4.7	1.3*
IS iv	Paraphrasing materials	4.3	1.5*
IS v	Skimming or scan reading text	4.5	2.4
IS vi	Summarising comment	4.5	1.5*
IS vii	Mis-reading text	0.8	2.3*
IS viii	Interpreting text	3.5	0.7*
IS ix	Misinterpreting text	0.2	1.8
IS x	Assessing relevance of information to the task	3.4	1.3*
IS xi	Assessing some other aspect of information	2.5	5.1*
IS xii	Marking and selecting relevant information	5.3	3.4

During information sampling, we find more differences between the two groups. Some differences, while seemingly large, will not of course approach significance if the standard deviation is high. Good students carry out a detailed read more frequently than poor students, which may act to reduce the frequency with which they then need to re-read materials. Good students focus, paraphrase, interpret and summarise materials more frequently than poorer students. In short, they are more active in building an understanding of the text than are poor students. Poor students occasionally mis-read the text. Good students more frequently assess the relevance of the materials to the task, whereas poor students tend to assess some other aspect of the materials, such as intrinsic interest, without regard for the task.

Planning and execution		Good students	Poor students
PE i	Planning structure of essay	1.7	0.3*
PE ii	Inclusion of marked relevant text	3.5	1.4*
PE iii	Inclusion of non-marked text	1.3	4.1*
PE iv	Monitoring progress in writing	2.4	1.1*
PE v	Reading over what has been written	1.6	0.8
PE vi	Evaluating what has been written	1.4	0.2*
PE vii	Evaluating overall response to the task	1.5	0.6
Metacomments		2.4	1.2
Miscellaneous		2.6	4.2

During planning and execution, good students plan their essay and include materials that have been assessed as relevant to the task more frequently than poorer students. Poorer students include material that has been assessed on other task irrelevant criteria, and fail to monitor their progress in writing. Finally, good students evaluate what they have written.

Task B

Again, recall that Task B comprised three broad phases of activity. These were:

- Task definition
- Comprehension
- Planning and execution

The behaviours specific to each phase are outlined below, with frequency data for each group of students:

Task definition		Good students	Poor students
TD i	Reading instructions	1.2	1.1
TD ii	Re-reading instructions	1.2	0.3
TD iii	Interpreting instructions	1.2	0.6*
TD iv	Goal definition	2.3	0.7*

Frequency data (mean)

During task definition, we find a similar pattern of results again. Good students interpret instructions and define goals more frequently than poorer students.

During the comprehension phase, good students again appear to engage more frequently in activities that centre on understanding the argument presented to them. Poorer students more frequently misinterpret the text and the reasoning contained within the text. Good students tend to evaluate the reasoning within the text, while poorer students simply comment on the reasoning presented. Good students more frequently generate new arguments.

Finally, during planning and execution, good students monitor and evaluate their writing more frequently than poor students. Poor students are more likely simply to re-state the argument that has been presented and are less likely to evaluate their own reasoning.

4 Analysing verbal protocol data

Comprehension		Good students	Poor students
C i	Detailed read	3.5	2.7
C ii	Re-reading	3.2	4.2
C iii	Focusing	1.2	0.6
C iv	Paraphrasing from the passage	2.1	0.7*
C v	Skimming or scan reading text	0.9	0.4
C vi	Summarising comment	2.6	1.1*
C vii	Mis-reading text	1.1	2.6
C viii	Interpreting text	2.2	0.7*
C ix	Misinterpreting text	0.9	2.6*
C x	Evaluating reasoning	4.6	2.1*
C xi	Expressing agreement or disagreement	1.2	2.5*
C xii	Misinterpreting argument	1.2	2.1*
C xiii	Generating a new argument	3.5	0.7*

Planning and execution		Good students	Poor students
PE i	Planning structure of essay	2.1	0.3
PE ii	Re-stating the presented argument	2.0	3.2*
PE iii	Evaluating the content or topic of an argument	3.5	0.6*
PE iv	Generating a statement (unsupported)	1.2	2.2*
PE v	Monitoring progress in writing	2.2	0.5*
PE vi	Reading over what has been written	2.4	0.4*
PE vii	Evaluating what has been written	2.2	0.8
PE viii	Evaluating overall response to the task	2.7	1.1
Metacomments		3.8	1.6
Miscellaneous		1.1	1.8

Summary

To summarise, we find interesting patterns emerging from the analysis of the protocols. The predictions made about performance of good and poor students were largely borne out by the data. We also find that there are some similarities between the two tasks in that good students adopt a more structured

4 Analysing verbal protocol data

approach to the tasks and more regularly monitor their progress on the tasks than do poorer students. Thus, we may be able to distinguish some general attributes of good writers from task-specific variables that distinguish among writers.

Example 2

Marker strategies in assessing CAE compositions

The following sections continue the discussion of the issues encountered in coding and analysing the data gathered for the marker strategies project.

Coding the protocols

The protocols were coded by two coders. Both had been involved in developing the coding scheme and both were therefore familiar with the coding categories. Protocols in this case were coded by hand and coded data were then transferred to computer file.

Some examples of actual codings are presented below. In this particular study, the researchers indicated codes associated with lines of protocol. Thus, in the first example below, line 113 includes several distinct activities. The first activity is an instance of detailed reading (A2i), followed by an evaluation of layout (B3vi), which is a positive response (coded 3).

Coder 1, Candidate A	Lines
[A2i B3vi {3}]	113
[A2i B4vii {1}]	113–121
[A2ii B3vii {1} B4vii {1}]	121
[A3i]	122
[A3v]	122

Coder 1, Candidate B	Lines
[A1i B3vi {1}]	98
[A2i B4iv {1}]	98–106
[A2ii B4iv {3} B2iv {1} B3vi {3}]	106–107
[A2i]	107
[A2ii B4i {1}]	107–108
[A4vi]	108
[A3v]	108

4 Analysing verbal protocol data

Coder 1, Candidate C	Lines
[A2i]	84–89
[A4vi]	89–90
[A2i]	90–92
[A2ii B4iv {3}]]	92–93
[A3v]]	93
[(D)]	93

Conventions with regard to use of symbols, use of line numbers and so forth are up to the individual researcher. It is worth pointing out again that consistency is very important in the use of symbols and conventions for coding protocols, since codes will frequently be submitted to various software packages for analysis.

Establishing encoder reliability

The full set of protocols were coded by both coders, and so encoder reliability was established by comparing the codings used in both instances. The proportion of occasions where the coders agreed was calculated and reliability estimated at greater than 80%. Individual reliability estimates for each code were not calculated in this example.

Data analysis

The study sought to identify the decision-making processes of examiners marking EFL compositions. To recap, the questions to be addressed were:

(i) Is it possible to abstract a model of good marking behaviour? What distinguishes good examiners from poorer examiners?
(ii) What influences rater consistency?
(iii) Do raters adjust their marking behaviour according to the level of the script?

Data were first analysed using a program which was developed specifically to gather frequency information. The program counted the frequency with which each of the different main groups was used by each examiner and also the frequency with which each of the subsidiary categories within each group was used. Evaluative comments were also counted.

In order to answer question (i), good examiners must be distinguished

4 Analysing verbal protocol data

from the less effective examiners. Once this has been done, protocols may be analysed in order to identify the correlates of good marking.

In this particular study, inter-examiner correlation coefficients were computed. This provided a matrix of correlational data for each examiner across the set of scripts. Correlations of above 0.7 were considered to be adequate. Correlations below this suggest a poor standard of assessment. The average overall correlation was computed for each examiner. This enabled the examiners to be grouped as follows:

Good examiners (average correlation above 0.77): total 8
Average examiners (average correlation between 0.70 and 0.77): total 5
Poor examiners (average correlation below 0.70): total 7

The initial analyses sought to identify at a very macro level differences between the three groups of examiners in the use of the two main coding categories (marking behaviour and factors noted by marker) and in the frequency and nature of the evaluative comments. These calculations give an indication of gross variations between the groups in general activities, such as reading the scripts, marking, attending to language and attending to technical features. Across all three groups, examiners' behaviour was dominated by attendance to the linguistic, task and technical factors of Category A. This difference was most pronounced among the poorer examiners.

Next, the four subcategories making up each of the two main category groups were considered and data were analysed at this more detailed level. This yielded eight categories across which to compare examiners and scripts. We begin by presenting the group observations (%) by script level data:

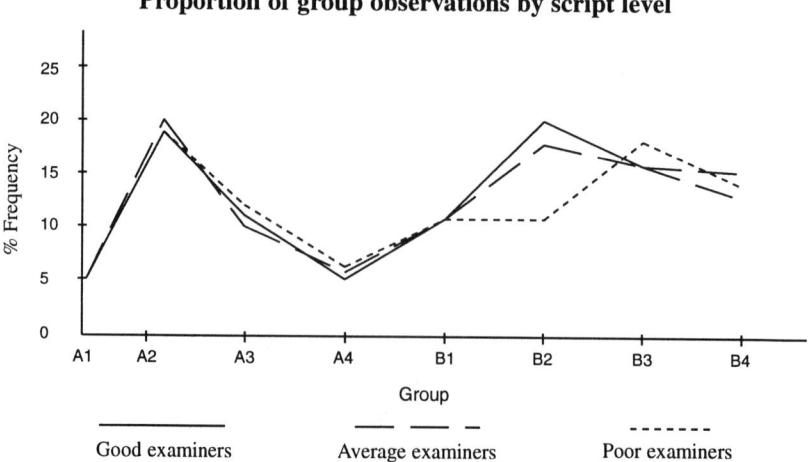

**Figure 10:
Proportion of group observations by script level**

4 Analysing verbal protocol data

The examiner profiles, averaged over individuals within each group, for good, average and poor scripts are shown in each of the three figures below:

**Figure 11(a):
Proportion of group observations for the three examiner groups
(good scripts)**

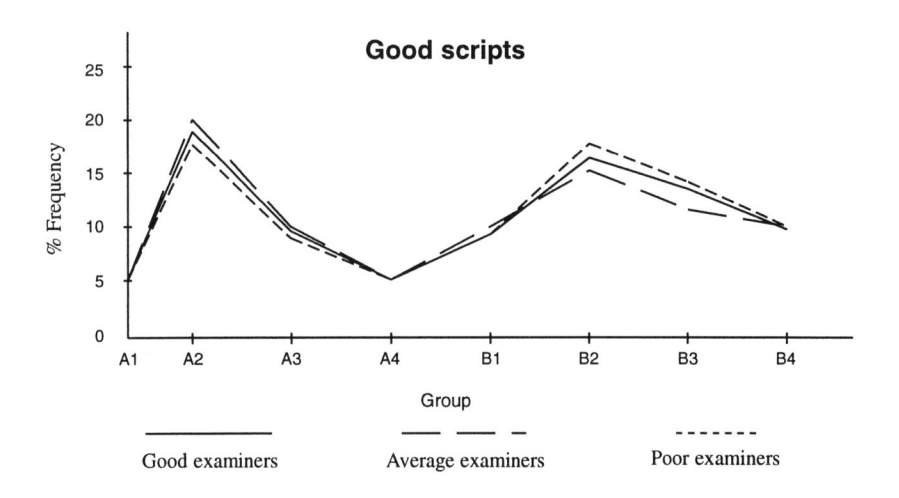

**Figure 11(b):
Proportion of group observations for the three examiner groups
(average scripts)**

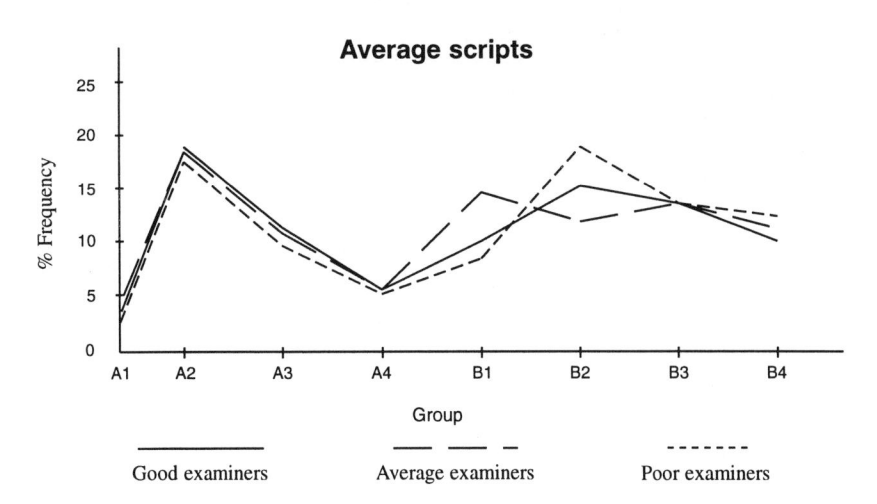

113

4 Analysing verbal protocol data

Figure 11(c):
Proportion of group observations for the three examiner groups (poor scripts)

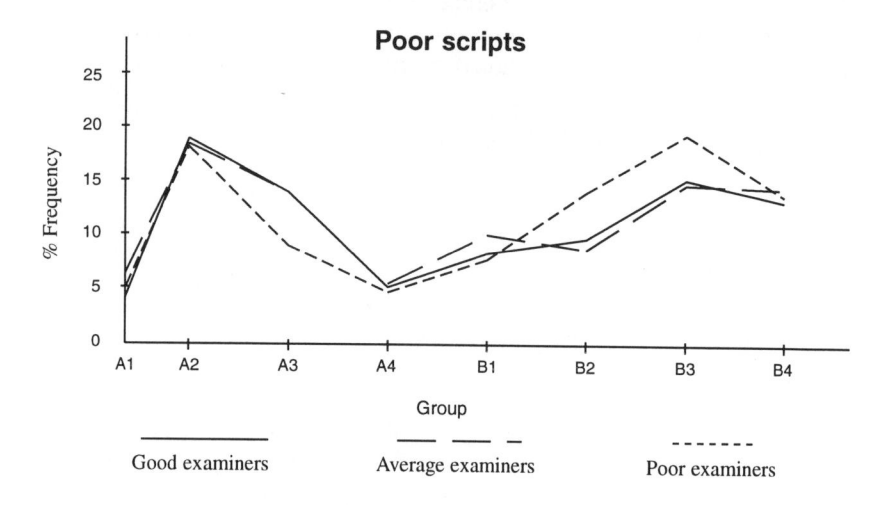

[Line graph titled "Poor scripts" showing % Frequency (0–25) on the y-axis against Group categories A1, A2, A3, A4, B1, B2, B3, B4 on the x-axis, with three lines representing Good examiners (solid), Average examiners (dashed), and Poor examiners (dotted).]

Irrespective of examiner skill level and script level, we can see that the differences between examiners on the Category A behaviour classes are very small and not significant. The main differences lie with the Category B behaviour classes. In the case of good scripts, the most marked differences centre on B2 (language appropriateness) and B3 (technical language features). For average scripts, we find the same trend with regard to B2 behaviour, although it is more marked here. The differences between examiners' B1 and B4 behaviour are most pronounced with the average scripts. Finally, good and average examiners exhibited very similar marking profiles for poor scripts. Poor examiners show more B2 and B3 behaviours, and some Category A differences emerge, poorer examiners engaging less in actual reading and marking behaviours.

Next, each individual coding category making up the four groups within each of the main two coding groups was examined. At this microscopic level of analysis, the behavioural patterns of individual examiners are more readily discernible, although the resulting complex profiles can be more difficult to interpret. Any differences that may not be apparent at more aggregate levels should be revealed at this level of analysis. Since there are quite a number of individual categories at this level, we shall focus on categories where differences between script levels emerged. These differences are summarised in Figure 12.

4 Analysing verbal protocol data

Figure 12:
Main differences at each individual category level for the three script levels

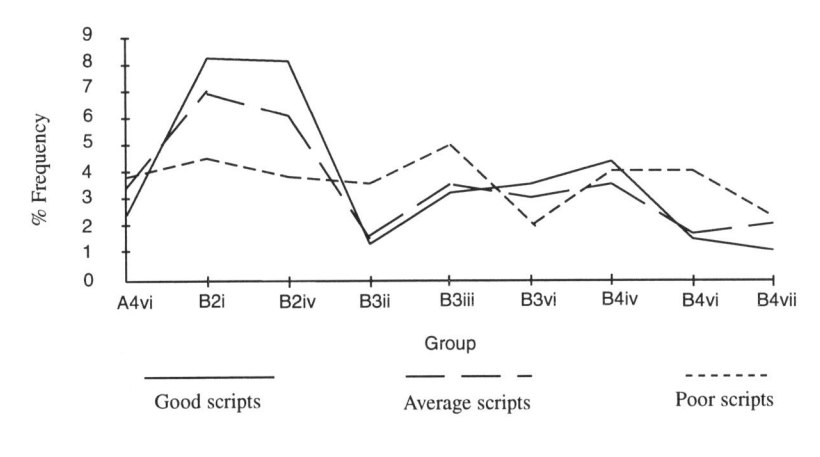

[Graph: % Frequency vs Group (A4vi, B2i, B2iv, B3ii, B3iii, B3vi, B4iv, B4vi, B4vii) showing three lines: Good scripts, Average scripts, Poor scripts]

Key:

A4vi	Marking attitude	B3vi	Layout
B2i	Register	B4iv	Content
B2iv	Style	B4vi	Task completion
B3ii	Spelling accuracy	B4vii	Understanding
B3iii	Grammar accuracy		

The differences can be interpreted as follows. Good scripts elicit attention to details such as register, style, layout and content. Examiners focus less on these features as script quality declines. Instead, they focus more on composition elements, such as spelling and grammatical accuracy, task understanding and task completion.

Finally, we consider differences between examiners of different skill levels in terms of their responses to scripts at each of the three levels. Poor examiners appear to spend less time reviewing marks awarded for high level scripts than did average and good examiners. Poor examiners also focus more on register and expression than do average and good examiners. Average examiners attend to the format of high level scripts more than do poor and good examiners.

As script quality declines to average, so the attention to reviewing marking increases for the good examiners. The difference in weighting given to format by average examiners is present, but less pronounced than it was for the good scripts. Poor examiners still focus more on expression within the scripts, whereas other examiners substantially reduce attention to this detail.

Even with the poorest scripts, good examiners still attend more to marking review than do the other examiners. Poor examiners continue to attend to register, whereas the good examiners have modified their behaviour, reducing attention to this element.

Summary

This worked example illustrates some of the ways in which a set of verbal protocols may be analysed. The analyses were performed at different levels of granularity, commencing by contrasting categories of behaviours and then becoming increasingly detailed, focusing eventually upon the individual behaviours themselves.

Summary

The two worked examples are informative in quite distinct ways. The first worked example reveals differences between writers of different abilities on both tasks, and also highlights some more generalisable attributes of good writing. The coding scheme is able to capture these general characteristics by using some of the same coding categories.

The second worked example illustrates the advantages in using hierarchical coding schemes. Patterns among examiners at different levels of granularity may then be discerned. Often, interesting differences between individuals or groups of individuals emerge at these quite detailed levels of analysis.

Tutorial exercise

This is a much more loosely designed exercise than those previously presented. We suggest that you gather some verbal protocols from a small group of individuals carrying out a familiar and well-defined task. Reading might be a suitable task, or cloze completion. Develop a coding scheme for the protocols and analyse the data. Try out some of the techniques suggested in this chapter, such as profiling and comparing groups. It may also be instructive to experiment with more than one coding scheme in order to assess which provides the most useful information.

5 Overview and future directions

The preceding chapters sought to provide a detailed description of the methodology of verbal protocol analysis, providing examples to illustrate the different steps in applying the procedure. Each chapter has attempted to explore a range of different issues encountered at each stage in using the methodology.

We have shown that the technique of protocol analysis may be used to gather information during the process of construct validation. Messick (1989) points out that different inferences may be made from test scores, and that in order to do this, the researcher requires validity evidence from a variety of sources. The source of evidence with which this volume has been most concerned has been that derived from analyses of processes, and specifically, evidence for cognitive processes which may be obtained from verbal protocols.

Since construct validation is an important phase in the development of any test, protocol analysis need not be seen as a methodology that applies solely to the domain of language testing – it may usefully be used in other assessment domains. For instance, Green (1994) used verbal protocols to help identify the range of strategies and processes used by students solving mathematical reasoning problems.

One of the most useful aspects of the methodology, which we noted in Chapter 1, is its ability to capture the dynamic nature of skilled performance. A verbal protocol produced by an individual working over a period of time provides a wealth of information on the cognitive processes used to carry out the task, information heeded as the task is carried out, but more importantly, changes occurring in both. Thus, we can observe the development of strategies and changes in the use of knowledge as the individual becomes more skilled. As our understanding of construct validation develops and becomes ever more sophisticated, so it becomes clearer that methods used as part of any process of construct validation must incorporate notions of dynamic constructs. Simply put, the same test given to individuals differing in level of skill development is quite likely to measure different aspects of skilled performance for those individuals. Nowhere is this more apparent than when we compare experts with novices. Differences between experts and novices are

5 Overview and future directions

not merely quantitative, but there are significant qualitative differences too. Thus, as skill develops, individuals not only cope with increasingly more complex tasks from the domain in question, but the manner in which information is processed also changes, becoming increasingly schema-based. Assessing a construct of emergent expertise requires instruments sensitive to the changes in knowledge structures and cognitive processes that accompany skill development in the domain in question.

The second chapter focused on data collection and preparation, and showed that verbal protocols may be used at a number of stages in test development to address different issues. Protocol analysis then is a widely applicable and powerful methodology. Chapter 2 considered characteristics of tasks that render them either suitable or not suitable for a protocol study. What is impressive is the wide range of tasks that do lend themselves to further examination through verbal protocol analysis. The broad applicability of the technique does not in any way imply that ensuing analyses may lack depth or precision. The power of the technique derives from the applicability of the coding scheme.

Deciding whether to use verbal protocol analysis and selecting an appropriate procedure are both relatively easy matters. As we saw in Chapter 3, the most difficult stage is the development of the coding scheme. Opting for inappropriate categories immediately reduces the effectiveness of the analysis, and may even invalidate it. Because coding schemes must be developed to suit the situation at hand, checking the reliability of encodings is crucial. The same observations hold for establishing the reliability of encodings of verbal protocols as apply to establishing reliability in the domain of testing – increasing the range of categories that may be used generally reduces estimates of reliability. We redress the problem to some extent when using verbal protocol data, by obtaining estimates of agreement within each coding category.

Most researchers who embark on protocol analysis take great care in applying appropriate statistical tests. We examined just a few of the approaches to statistical analysis of coded data in Chapter 4. Sometimes, verbal protocol data are not well analysed. This can be highly problematic. Even if the data collection procedures and coding scheme are adequate, weak analytical methods will mask the information contained within the protocols. Verbal protocol data require careful and extensive analysis. This is hardly surprising when we consider that verbal protocols are an immensely rich source of data.

A discussion of the use of verbal protocols within any context would not be complete without consideration of the merits of such qualitative approaches and their place beside the more conventional quantitative approaches. Criticisms of protocol analysis were considered earlier. The information processing paradigm, which predominates within psychology, allows researchers to explicate the processes and knowledge required to perform various tasks. The level of detail demanded in order to construct computer

5 Overview and future directions

simulations of performance on a range of tasks ensures that models are explicit and powerful. Subjectivity in the use of protocol analysis is thus minimised. Throughout this volume, we have seen that verbal reports are a valid and useful source of data in their own right.

Cohen (1996) considers some issues in the use of verbal protocols for L2 researchers. Concurrent protocols are of course just that, but other procedures involve some delay between actually carrying out the task and providing the verbal report. Studies purportedly using these non-concurrent techniques show some variation in time that elapses between task completion and the generation of the verbal report. Differences in the immediacy with which verbal reports are produced complicate matters, since as we saw earlier, retrospective reports can be prone to unwanted interference from other cognitive processes. This underlines the requirements for special care in eliciting verbal reports from subjects. One of the problems in introducing a new methodology, and especially one that is susceptible to interference, is that researchers may quickly adopt the general ideas but forget to pay sufficient attention to the specific details. Any insights gained may be of limited use and subtle procedural variations may make it difficult to compare findings from superficially similar studies.

Is verbal protocol analysis likely to prove a valuable methodology for researchers in language testing? To the extent that verbal protocols are a useful source of information that may be used as part of the process of construct validation, then the methodology may have much to recommend it. Verbal protocols uniquely provide information on the cognitive processes and heeded information used in carrying out a given task. Cumming (1996) notes the importance of validation work in language assessment. Some researchers in this area are already using verbal protocols as part of the construct validation process (Wijgh 1996; Milanovic and Saville 1994).

The methodology of content analysis has been used extensively in language testing research. Bachman, Davidson and Milanovic (1996) discuss the role of content validation in the development of test specifications. Their discussion makes a number of important points, perhaps none more so than the observation that we need an understanding of the test methods that are used to measure the abilities in question. Thus, information about test content is not in itself sufficient – test developers also require an understanding of the test methods that are used. A particularly interesting venture then would be to use content analysis with protocol analysis to provide both quantitative and qualitative data on the relationship between test content and the performance of test takers.

One of the main goals of education is to impart knowledge and skills. However, one of the difficulties with traditional, more psychometric approaches is the implicit assumption that skills are 'unidimensional'. By this

5 Overview and future directions

is meant that an entire skill is taken to be the unit for analysis. Thus, according to the unidimensional view, 'reading' might be considered a unitary skill, as might 'spelling'. Mislevy (1989) points out that the unidimensionality assumption, which underlies item response theory and other theories, is at odds with what we have learned about the nature of skills and their acquisition from cognitive psychology. For instance, reading is a highly complex skill, involving a range of distinct processes, each making its own contribution. Knowledge does not just accumulate with learning, but it changes in form and structure. Domain-relevant knowledge structures develop and reconfigure with skill development. Increasingly specific domain-relevant strategies are also acquired and refined as skill develops. Verbal protocol analysis is one means by which these changes may be directly observed and captured.

Verbal protocol analysis, like other methodologies, provides us with a means for both testing and developing theories. In the context of language testing, it has the potential to elucidate the abilities that need to be measured, and also to provide a means for identifying relevant test methods and selecting appropriate test content.

Protocol analysis should not be seen merely as a method to be used as part of construct validation, but should also be viewed as a means by which we may enrich our understanding of the very nature of the construct(s) under investigation. Furthermore, the oft noted criticism of construct validation, that it is frequently carried out *a posteriori*, may be redressed through the increased use of verbal protocols. Verbal protocols offer scope for specifying *a priori* (through task analysis and the development of a coding scheme) the cognitive processes and knowledge that underpin the ability that is to be measured.

References

Anderson, J. R., Farrell, R. and Sauers, R. 1984. Learning to program in LISP. *Cognitive Science* 8, 87–129.

Bachman, L. F. 1990. *Fundamental Considerations in Language Testing*. University Press.

Bachman, L. F., Davidson, F. and Milanovic, M. 1996. The use of test method characteristics in the content analysis and design of EFL Proficiency tests. *Language Testing* 13, 125–151.

Ballstaedt, S. P. and Mandl, H. 1984. Elaborations: Assessment and analysis. In H. Mandl, N. L. Stein and T. Trabasso (eds.), *Learning and Comprehension of Text*. Hillsdale, NJ: Lawrence Erlbaum Associates.

Bereiter, C. and Scardamalia, M. 1985. Cognitive coping strategies and the problem of 'inert knowledge'. In S. F. Chipman, J. W. Segal and R. Glaser (eds.), *Thinking and Learning Skills*, Vol. 2: Current research and open questions. Hillsdale, NJ: Lawrence Erlbaum Associates.

Bereiter, C. and Scardamalia, M. 1987. *The Psychology of Written Composition*. Hillsdale, NJ: Lawrence Erlbaum Associates.

Bhaskar, R. and Simon, H. R. 1977. Problem solving in semantically rich domains: An example from engineering thermodynamics. *Cognitive Science* 1, 193–215.

Buck, G. 1992. *The Testing of Second Language Listening Comprehension*. Unpublished PhD. thesis. University of Lancaster, England.

Chi, M. T. H., Glaser, R. and Rees, E. 1982. Expertise in problem solving. In R. J. Sternberg (ed.), *Advances in the Psychology of Human Intelligence*. Hillsdale, NJ: Lawrence Erlbaum Associates.

Cohen, A. D. 1996. Towards enhancing verbal reports as a source of insights on test-taking strategies. Paper presented at Language Testing Research Colloquium (LTRC), Finland, July 31–August 3, 1996.

Cronbach, L. J. and Meehl, P. G. 1955. Construct validity in psychological tests. *Psychological Bulletin* 52, 281–302.

Cumming, A. 1996. Introduction: The concept of validation in language testing. Validation in language testing. *Modern Languages in Practice 2*, 1–14. Great Britain: Cromwell Press.

References

Deville, C. and Chalhoub-Deville, M. 1993. Modified scoring, traditional item analysis and SATO's caution index used to investigate the reading recall protocol. *Language Testing* 10 (2), 117–132.

Diederich, P. B., French, J. and Carlton, S. 1961. Factors in judgements of writing ability. *ETS Research Bulletin* RB-61-15. Princeton, NJ: Educational Testing Service.

Ericsson, K. A. 1988. Concurrent verbal reports on reading and text comprehension. *Text 8* (4), 295–325.

Ericsson, K. A. and Simon, H. 1993. *Protocol Analysis*. Cambridge, Mass: MIT Press.

Flower, L. S. and Hayes, J. R. 1980. The dynamics of composing: Making plans and juggling constraints. L. W. Gregg and E. R. Steinberg (eds.), *Cognitive Processes in Writing*. Hillsdale, NJ: Lawrence Erlbaum Associates.

Freedle, R. and Kostin, I. 1993. The prediction of TOEFL reading item difficulty: Implications for construct validity. *Language Testing*, 10 (2), 133–70.

Freedman, S. 1979. How characteristics of student essays influence teachers' evaluation. *Journal of Educational Psychology*, 71, 328–338.

Gerloff, P. 1987. Identifying the unit of analysis in translation: Some uses of think-aloud protocol data. In C. Faerch and G. Kasper (eds.), *Introspection in Second Language Research*. Clevedon, Avon: Multilingual Matters Ltd.

Gilhooly, K. J. 1986. Individual differences in thinking aloud performance. *Current Psychological Research and Reviews* 5 (4), 328–34.

Gilhooly, K. J. and Green, C. 1989. A suite of computer programs for use in verbal protocol analysis. *Literary and Linguistic Computing* 4, 1–5.

Green, A. J. K. 1994. Interacting cognitive subsystems: framework for considering the relationships between performance and knowledge representations. *Interacting with Computers* 6 (1), 61–85.

Green, A. J. K. and Gilhooly, K. J. 1990a. Statistical computing: Individual differences in learning at microscopic and macroscopic levels. In K. J. Gilhooly, R. H. Logie, M. T. G. Keane and G. Erdos (eds.), *Lines of Thinking: Reflections on the Psychology of Thought*. Chichester, UK: Wiley.

Green, A. J. K. and Gilhooly, K. J. 1990b. Individual differences and effective learning procedures: The case of statistical computing. *International Journal of Man-Machine Studies* 33, 97–119.

Green, A. J. K. and Gilhooly, K. J. 1992. Empirical advances in expertise research. In M. T. Keane and K. J. Gilhooly (eds.), *Advances in the Psychology of Thinking* 1. London, UK: Harvester Wheatsheaf.

Grobe, C. 1981. Syntactic maturity, mechanics and vocabulary as predictors of quality ratings. *Research in the Teaching of English* 15, 75–86.

References

Hayes-Roth, B. and Hayes-Roth, F. 1987. A cognitive model of planning. *Cognitive Science*, 3, 275–310.

Hölscher, A. and Möhle, D. 1987. Cognitive plans in translation. In C. Faerch and G. Kasper (eds.), *Introspection in Second Language Research*. Clevedon, Avon: Multilingual Matters Ltd.

Laszlo, Jr., Meutsch, D. and Viehoff, R. 1988. Verbal reports as data in text comprehension research: An introduction. *Text* 8, 283–94.

Lazaraton, A. 1996. A qualitative approach to monitoring examiner conduct in the Cambridge Assessment of Spoken English (CASE). In M. Milanovic and N. Saville (eds.).

Messick, S. 1989. Validity. In R. L. Linn (ed.), *Educational Measurement* (3rd Edition). Washington DC: American Council on Education/ Macmillan Series on Higher Education.

Milanovic, M. and Saville, N. 1994. An investigation of marking strategies using verbal protocols. Paper presented at Language Testing Research Colloquium, March 1994.

Milanovic, M., and Saville, N (eds.). 1996. *Performance Testing, Cognition and Assessment:* Selected Papers from the 15th Language Testing Research Colloquium (LTRC), Cambridge and Arnhem. Cambridge: University of Cambridge Local Examinations Syndicate and Cambridge University Press.

Milanovic, M., Saville, N. and Shen, S. 1992. An exploratory study of markers' decision-making behaviour in evaluating FCE/CPE paper 2 compositions. EFL Evaluation Unit internal report, University of Cambridge Local Examinations Syndicate.

Milanovic, M., Saville, N. and Shen, S. 1996. A study of the decision-making behaviour of composition markers. In M. Milanovic and N. Saville (eds.).

Milanovic, M. 1997. A common European framework of reference for Language Learning and Teaching, *User's Guide for Examiners*. Strasbourg: Council of Europe.

Mislevy, R. J. 1989. Foundations of a new test theory. *ETS Research Report*. Princeton, NJ: Educational Testing Service.

Nisbett, R. E. and Wilson, T. D. 1977. Telling more than we can know: Verbal reports on mental processes. *Psychological Review* 84, 231–59.

Norman, D. A. 1981. Categorization of action slips. *Psychological Review* 88, 1–15.

Norman, D. A. 1988. *The Design of Everyday Things*. New York: Doubleday.

Norris, S. P. 1991. Informal reasoning assessment: Using verbal reports of thinking to improve multiple-choice test validity. In J. F. Voss, D. N. Perkins and J. W. Segal (eds.), *Informal Reasoning and Education*. Hillsdale, NJ: Lawrence Erlbaum Associates.

Payne, S. and Squibb, H. 1990. Algebra mal-rules and cognitive accounts of error. *Cognitive Science* 14, 445–81.

References

Reason, J. 1979. Actions not as planned: The price of automatization. In G. Underwood and K. Stevens (eds.), *Aspects of Consciousness*, Vol. 1, 67–90. London and San Diego: Academic Press.

Scardamalia, M. and Bereiter, C. 1985. Fostering the development of self-regulation in children's knowledge processing. In S. F. Chipman, J. W. Segal and R. Glaser (eds.), *Thinking and Learning Skills*, Vol. 2: Current research and open questions. Hillsdale, NJ: Lawrence Erlbaum Associates.

Schoenfeld, A. H. 1983. Episodes and executive decisions in mathematical problem solving. In R. Lesh and M. Landau (eds.), *Acquisition of Maths Concepts and Processes*. New York: Academic Press.

Schoenfeld, A. H. and Herrmann, D. J. 1982. Problem perception and knowledge structure in expert and novice mathematical problem solvers. *Journal of Experimental Psychology: Learning, Memory and Cognition* 8 (5), 484–94.

Schvaneveldt, R. W., Durso, F. T., Goldsmith, T. E., Breen, T. J., Cooke, N. M., Tucker, R. G., and De Maio, J. C. 1985. Measuring the structure of expertise. *International Journal of Man-Machine Studies* 23, 699–728.

Shohamy, E. and Inbar, O. 1991. Validation of listening comprehension tests: The effect of text and questions type. *Language Testing* 8, 23–40.

Stewart, M. and Grobe, C. 1979. Syntactic maturity, mechanics of writing and teacher's quality ratings. *Research in the Teaching of English* 13, 207–15.

Thorndyke, P. W. and Stasz, C. 1980. Individual differences in procedures for knowledge acquisition from maps. *Cognitive Psychology* 12, 137–75.

Upshur. J. A., 1979. Functional proficiency theory and a research role for language tests. In E. J. Brière and F. B. Hinofotis (eds.), *Concepts in Language Testing: Some Recent Studies*. Washington, DC: TESOL.

University of Cambridge Local Examinations Syndicate. 1995. Paper 1, Reading. *FCE Specifications and Sample Papers for the Revised FCE Examination* (2nd edition).

University of Cambridge Local Examinations Syndicate. 1995. Paper 2, Writing. *CPE Handbook*.

Voss, J. F., Greene, T. R., Post, T. A. and Penner, B. C. 1983. Problem solving skill in the social sciences. In G. Bower (ed.), *The Psychology of Learning and Motivation* (Vol. 17). New York: Academic Press.

Wijgh, I. F. 1996. A communicative test in analysis: strategies in reading authentic texts. Validation in language testing. *Modern Languages in Practice 2*, 154–70. Great Britain: Cromwell Press.

Wood, R. 1991. *Assessment and Testing*. Cambridge: Cambridge University Press.

APPENDIX I

PAPER 1 – READING

Appendix I

Paper 1 – Reading

Paper Format The paper contains 4 parts. Each part contains a text and corresponding comprehension tasks. One part may contain 2 or more shorter related texts.

Length of Texts 1900–2300 words approximately overall; 350–700 words approximately per text.

Numbers of Questions 35.

Text Types From the following: advertisements, correspondence, fiction, informational material (e.g. brochures, guides, manuals, etc.) messages, newspaper and magazine articles, reports.

Task Types Gapped text, multiple choice, multiple matching.

Task Focus Understanding gist, main points, detail, text structure or specific information, or deducing meaning.

Answering For all parts of this paper, candidates indicate their answers by shading the correct lozenges on an answer sheet.

Timing 1 hour 15 minutes.

Appendix I

Part	Task Type and Focus	Number of Questions	Task Format
1	Multiple matching Focus as for whole paper	6 or 7	A text preceded by multiple matching questions. Candidates must match a prompt from one list to a prompt in another list, or match prompts to elements in the text.
2	Multiple choice Focus as for whole paper	7 or 8	A test followed by four-option multiple choice questions.
3	Gapped text Understanding gist, main points, detail and text structure	6 or 7	A text from which paragraphs or sentences have been removed and placed in jumbled order after the text. Candidates must decide from where in the text the paragraphs or sentences have been removed.
4	Multiple matching, Multiple choice	13–15	As Part 1.

Appendix I

PART 1

You are going to read a magazine article about car theft. Choose the most suitable heading from the list **A–I** for each part (**1–7**) of the article. There is one extra heading which you do not need to use. There is an example at the beginning (**0**).
Mark your answers **on the separate answer sheet**.

A		Watch where you park.
B		Car crime increase.
C		Large car parks are safer.
D		Will you get it back?
E		Three minutes is all it takes.
F		One in ten invites thieves.
G		Take it with you.
H		A million cars are at risk.
I		Take the keys with you.

Appendix I

An expensive business

As car crime soars, DAVID ROWLANDS and CHRISTOPHER JONES plot the rise of car theft in Britain

0 I

A million motorists leave their cars full up with petrol and with the keys in the ignition every day.

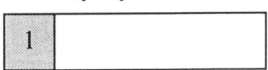

1

The vehicles are sitting in petrol stations while drivers pay for their fuel. The Automobile Association (AA) has discovered that cars are left unattended for an average three minutes – and sometimes considerably longer – as drivers buy drinks, sweets, cigarettes and other consumer items – and then pay at the cash till. With payment by credit card more and more common, it is not unusual for a driver to be out of his car for as long as six minutes, providing the car thief with a golden opportunity.

2

In an exclusive AA survey, carried out at a busy garage on a main road out of London, 300 motorists were questioned over three days of the holiday period. Twenty four per cent admitted that they 'always' or 'sometimes' leave the keys in their cars. This means that nationwide, a million cars daily become easy targets for the opportunist thief.

3

For more than ten years there has been a bigger rise in car crime than in most other types of crime. An average of more than two cars a minute are broken into, vandalised or stolen in the UK. Car crime accounts for almost a third of all reported offences with no signs that the trend is slowing down.

4

Although there are highly professional criminals involved in car theft, almost 90 per cent of car crime is committed by the opportunist. Amateur thieves are aided by our own carelessness. When AA engineers surveyed one town centre car park last year, ten per cent of the cars checked were unlocked, a figure backed by a Home Office national survey that found 12 per cent of drivers sometimes left their cars unlocked. The AA recommends locking up whenever you leave the car – and for however short a period. A partially open sunroof or window is a further come-on to thieves.

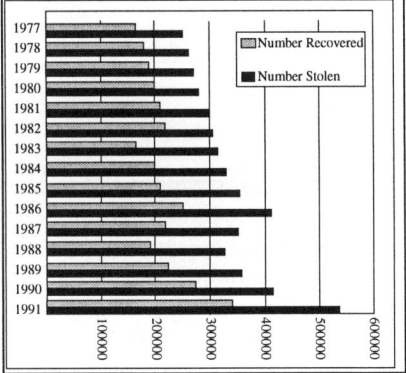

There are many other traps to avoid. The Home Office has found little awareness among drivers about safe parking. Most motorists questioned made no efforts to avoid parking in quiet spots away from street lights – just the places thieves love. The AA advises drivers to park in places with people around – thieves don't like audiences.

Leaving valuables in view is

6

an invitation to the criminal. A Manchester Probationary Service research project, which interviewed almost 100 car thieves last year, found many would investigate a coat thrown on a seat. Never leave any documents showing your home address in the car. If you have a garage, use it and lock it – a garaged car is at substantially less risk.

5

7

Appendix I

PART 2

You are going to read an extract from an autobiography. For questions **8–15**, choose the answer (**A, B, C** or **D**) which you think fits best according to the text. Mark your answers **on the separate answer sheet**.

My new home was a long way from the centre of London but it was becoming essential to find a job, so finally I spent a whole morning getting to town and putting my name down to be considered by London Transport for a job on the tube. They were looking for guards, not drivers. This suited me. I couldn't drive a car but thought that I could probably guard a train, and perhaps continue to write my poems between stations. The writers Keats and Chekhov had been doctors. T.S. Eliot had worked in a bank and Wallace Stevens for an insurance company. I would be a tube guard. I could see my myself being cheerful, useful, a good man in a crisis. Obviously I would be overqualified but I was willing to forget about that in return for a steady income and travel privileges – those latter being particularly welcome to someone living a long way from the city centre.

The next day I sat down, with almost a hundred other candidates for the intelligence test. I must have done all right because after half an hour's wait I was sent into another room for the psychological test. This time there were only about fifty candidates. The examiner sat at a desk. You were signalled forward to occupy the seat opposite him when the previous occupant had been dismissed, after a greater or shorter time. Obviously the long interviews were the more successful ones. Some of the interviews were as short as five minutes. Mine was the only one that lasted a minute and a half.

I can remember the questions now. 'Why did you leave your last job?' 'Why did you leave the job before that?' 'And the one before that?' I can't recall my answers, except that they were short at first and grew progressively shorter. His closing statement, I thought, revealed a lack of sensitivity which helped to explain why as a psychologist, he had risen no higher than the underground railway. 'You have failed the psychological test and we are unable to offer you a position.'

Failing to get that job was my low point. Or so I thought, believing that the work was easy. Actually, such jobs – being a postman is another one I still desire – demand exactly the sort of elementary yet responsible awareness that the habitual dreamer is least qualified to give. But I was still far short of full self-understanding. I was also short of cash.

Appendix I

8 Why did the writer apply for the job?

  A He could no longer afford to live without one.
  B He wanted to work in the centre of London.
  C He had suitable training.
  D He was not interested in any other available jobs.

9 It suited him to become a guard on the tube because

  A the job would be near his home.
  B he did not want too much responsibility.
  C it would give him the opportunity to write.
  D he did not have any other qualifications.

10 What quality did the writer think he would bring to the job of guard?

  A His intelligence would be useful to the organisation.
  B He was an experienced underground traveller.
  C He understood what the job required.
  D He would be able to deal with difficult situations.

11 What did he find especially attractive about the job?

  A He wanted to get to work more quickly.
  B He wanted to do a useful job.
  C He would be able to earn high wages.
  D He would be able to receive special benefits.

12 The length of his interview meant that

  A he had not done well in the intelligence test.
  B the job was not going to be offered to him.
  C he had little work experience to talk about.
  D the examiner had decided he didn't like him.

13 Why didn't he get the job?

  A He was too nervous to give proper answers.
  B He could not remember the answers to the questions.
  C His answers appeared to be unsatisfactory.
  D There were no more positions to be filled.

14 What was the writer's opinion of the psychologist?

  A He was inefficient at his job.
  B He was unsympathetic.
  C He was unhappy in his job.
  D He was very aggressive.

15 What does the writer realise now that he did not realise then?

  A how difficult it can be to get a job
  B how unpleasant ordinary jobs can be
  C how badly he did in the interview
  D how unsuitable he was for the job

Appendix I

PART 3

You are going to read a newspaper article about a singer. Seven sentences have been removed from the article. Choose from the sentences **A–H** the one which fits each gap (**16–21**). There is one extra sentence which you do not need to use. There is an example at the beginning (**0**).
Mark your answers **on the separate answer sheet.**

ROOM OF MY OWN
Interview by Ena Kendall

Najma Akhtar sings Indian love poems to a mixture of Eastern and Western rhythms and might seem an unlikely pop star. Yet since winning the Asian Song Contest in Birmingham in 1984, she has been praised round the world as well as in this country, where she was the first Asian singer to appear at London's premier jazz clubs, achieving a sell-out. Her music has its roots in the *ghazals* – love poems – and *gawwali* – hymns and wedding songs of the Urdu-speaking Muslims of India. **0 H**

She became a singer almost by accident. Her parents reacted with horror to the possibility of their daughter entering into the suspicious world of popular musicians and did their best to discourage her. Najma is British born, brought up within the Asian community.

In her mid-twenties, Najma still lives with her parents in a large flat on the fringes of London's West End. Her room is her bedroom, simple, functional. **16**

She also keeps here a *tampura*, an Indian droning instrument she practises on, and a Western *harmonium*.

Though music and the arts were much opposed by her parents, they bought her – with much unwillingness – a second-hand harmonium for £20 when she continued with music. Najma had fulfilled part of their ambitions by getting an MSc at the University of Aston and qualifying as a chemical engineer. **17**

She comes from a family of engineers. 'My father is electrical, my sister civil, my brother is doing industrial engineering and my mother is a cooking engineer – she engineers all our food.' **18**

In her room can also be seen the Asian Song Contest award she won in 1984, with a song she composed and recorded. Her father wasn't keen on her entering but, 'my mother was an ally', she says. **19**

After this, she concentrated on making *ghazals* more acceptable to a wider audience. 'People who understand Urdu will listen to the words, then to the voice, then to the melody.' **20**

She released her first British album, *Qareeb*, in 1987; later, music from this album was featured on a movie soundtrack. **21**

The Japanese gave her a pottery cat for good luck; it stands near her award for best vocalist of the year at the Asian Pop Awards in Birmingham. She has won this three times in succession. Her room is, in fact, full of presents from fans all over the world.

Najma respects the values her parents taught her but is very determined to make a success of her music and do what she wants with her life.

132

Appendix I

A   The win was a shock for the whole family.

B   Her mother is also her road manager and travels with her on all her international tours.

C   Most Asian families aim for their children to enter the professions: doctor, pharmacist, architect, lawyer, engineer; all these things are drummed into children.

D   After her second album, she had a big success with a series of concerts in Paris, and was subsequently asked by CBS to record her third album in Japan.

E   She has simple tastes but enjoys winning.

F   She has a pile of woolly toys on the bed suggesting echoes of childhood, though in fact they were largely bought at airports, during long waits for planes.

G   We decided to make the music and the voice more interesting to make up for not understanding the words.

H   She combines these influences with Western ideas, writing her own lyrics and music.

Appendix I

PART 4

You are going to read some information about some British cities.
For questions **22–23**, choose from the cities (**A–H**). Some of the cities may be chosen more than once. When more than one answer is required, these may be given in any order. There is an example at the beginning (**0**).
For questions **34** and **35**, choose the answer (**A, B, C** or **D**) which you think fits best according to the text.
Mark your answers **on the separate answer sheet**.

Which city or cities would you recommend for someone who:

likes visiting cathedrals?	**0**	**H**
enjoys visiting parks and gardens?	**22**	
is interested in ships?	**23**	
is interested in the history of trains?	**24**	
is interested in buying old objects?	**25**	
likes animals?	**26**	**27**
likes visiting castles?	**28**	**29**
wants a holiday by the sea?	**30**	**31**
is interested in the way the Romans lived?	**32**	**33**

34 Where has this text come from?

- **A** a tour programme
- **B** a history book
- **C** a tourist leaflet
- **D** a newspaper report

35 Why would someone read this text?

- **A** to help them decide which city to visit
- **B** to show them the way round a city
- **C** to tell them about a city they have visited
- **D** to find out how to get to a city

Appendix I

Intercity Centres

Nottingham [A]

Visit Nottingham's Tales of Robin Hood exhibition and be transported back to the 13th century. The medieval Castle affords panoramic views over the city and there are many modern attractions, too – theatres, cinemas, restaurants and exhibitions, plus one of the finest shopping centres and markets in the Midlands where you can buy some beautiful lace.

More information is available by contacting the City of Nottingham Tourist Information Centre on 011594 470661.

Bath [B]

Aquae Sulis as it was once known by the Romans is hidden behind the Georgian façades of this historical city.

Spend some time discovering about life in Roman days by visiting the original bath spa.

Or wander the more recent Georgian streets, full of antique markets and modern shops.

Discover more about Bath by phoning Tourist Information on 01225 462831.

Great Yarmouth [C]

Travel InterCity to Norwich and join a connecting service to Great Yarmouth. The sea front is alive with all manner of amusements and entertainments – as one would expect at such a popular resort.

If boats are your thing, you'll see fleets of them at the huge Marina Centre; after all, this is the gateway to the beautiful Norfolk Broads. The Maritime Museum contains imaginative displays of East Anglian coastal history – including a collection of toys and ornaments made by local seamen.

Other places of historical interest are the fourteenth century Tollhouse, with its dungeons, exhibits of local history and a brass-rubbing centre. On South Quay there's the Old Merchant's House, and the Elizabethan House Museum, which actually specialises in displays of nineteenth century domestic life and Lowestoft porcelain.

For more information about Great Yarmouth contact 01493 846345.

Weston-super-Mare [D]

Extensive sands, a spacious promenade and lively shopping centre combine to make Weston the premier resort of Avon. It's certainly an ideal holiday centre for exploring this area. Weston-super-Mare offers a balanced mixture of relaxation and entertainment.

Three miles of Atlantic coastline sands and attractive parks contrast with a whirl of entertainment, amusements and sporting activities. There's virtually something for all the family all year round.

Weston's two piers, constructed between 1867 and 1904, are a lasting monument to the town's popularity as a holiday centre. Today they serve to add a touch of Victorian/Edwardian grandeur to this otherwise modern resort.

Further information on Weston-super-Mare can be obtained on 01934 626838.

Glasgow [E]

Glasgow has been hailed as the European City of Culture for 1990. And there's certainly a wide variety for you to enjoy. Art, theatre, ballet, opera, classical music, rock and jazz – the list is endless.

There's an abundance of natural beauty to be found in over 70 parks and gardens. Loch Lomond and Loch Long are within easy reach of the city by local services. A warm welcome is extended to visitors through a wide range of hotels, restaurants and lively pubs.

Phone the Greater Glasgow Tourist Board for all enquiries and information on 0141 2044400.

Chester [F]

The Romans founded Chester, and even today visitors can see evidence of this ancient settlement in the form of archaeological remains and artefacts.

A most interesting way to view the town is to take a stroll along the surrounding fortified walls, overlooking the picturesque River Dee.

Perhaps Chester's most unique attraction is its rows of half timbered, double tiered shops, which date back to Tudor and Elizabethan times.

Children would probably prefer to visit the nearby Chester zoo. It's a great day out for everybody!

Find out more about Chester by contacting the Tourist Information Centre, Town

Appendix I

Hall, Northgate Street, Chester or phone 01244 313126.

Edinburgh — G

Scotland's capital is rich in historical heritage and culture. Visit the Castle and view the Scottish Crown Jewels. There are excellent shopping opportunities in world famous Princes Street. Edinburgh Zoo is the home of Scotland's largest animal collection – including many endangered species.

You'll find plenty to see and do amongst the many galleries, exhibitions, shows, and gardens which Edinburgh has to offer. Find out more by phoning Tourist Information on 0131 557 1700.

York — H

This city has seen many cultures come and go – from the Romans through to the Vikings. Indeed, visitors to the Jorvik Viking Centre can step back in time and see a superbly reconstructed Viking settlement.

Other sites include the medieval York Dungeon, with its authentic sounds, smells and lighting; and Victorian streets containing remnants of everyday life in York's more recent past.

The National Railway Museum is here in York. Its Great Railway Show celebrates the Railway Age from the 1820s to the present day.

No visit to York is complete without a tour of majestic York Minster, Europe's largest Gothic Cathedral.

If you'd like to know more about this great city, contact the Tourist Information Centre on 01904 62055.

Appendix I

PAPER 1 – READING
FIRST SAMPLE PAPER – ANSWER KEY

PART 1
1	E
2	H
3	B
4	F
5	A
6	G
7	D

PART 2
8	A
9	C
10	D
11	D
12	B
13	C
14	B
15	D

PART 3
16	F
17	C
18	B
19	A
20	G
21	D

PART 4
22	E
23	C
24	H
25	B
26/27	F, G in any order
28/29	A, G in any order
30/31	C, D in any order
32/33	B, F in any order
34	C
35	A

APPENDIX II

PAPER 2 – COMPOSITION

Appendix II

Paper 2 – Composition

Description From a choice of five tasks, two compositions – generally of about 350 words – are to be written in 2 hours. One task, the more transactional one, is shorter, at about 300 words.

Test Focus Using natural and specially written language in response to a variety of thematic or situational stimuli.

Tasks The topics are designed to generate a natural use of language in response to a variety of thematic or situational prompts, as appropriate to the examination level. The focus and nature of the prompts takes account of the international context of the examination.

The range of tasks includes a description, a discursive composition, a narrative, and a piece of writing appropriate to a specified context (e.g. formal letter, report, short articles, etc.). There is also a task based on optional reading as specified in the Examination Regulations for each year. The introduction of background reading texts as an alternative stimulus composition in 1984 was intended to encourage work on extended texts as a basis for the enrichment of language studies.

Assessment The five prompts provide five different tasks, each of which demands varying responses and techniques. Examiners assess task-realisation, organisation of material and range of vocabulary and structure. Within these criteria, they consider fulfilment of the task set: (i.e. its relevance and organisation as a whole and in terms of individual paragraphs) and the quality of the language used (i.e. the range and appropriateness of vocabulary and sentence structure; the correctness of grammatical construction, punctuation and spelling). The examiners assess each composition based on these considerations, bearing in mind the general scope and standard of the CPE. The impression mark for each composition is awarded out of 20.

Appendix II

The criteria for assessment are summarised as follows:

16–20	Ambitious in concept and approach with high-quality language use and minimal errors.
11–15	Natural and appropriate in style with few errors and some sophisticated language use; successful realisation of task.
8–10	Message communicated but errors noticeable; attempts at task not entirely successful.
5–7	Lack of language control shown by frequent basic errors; task only partly realised/rubric neglected.
0–4	Language breakdown; content irrelevant or too little for assessment.

Appendix II

Length	The length of answer required is stated for each task. For answers that are below the required length, the examiner adjusts the maximum mark and the mark given proportionately, e.g. a three-quarter length answer deserves three-quarters of the mark that would otherwise have been given. For answers that are over-length, the examiner draws a line at the approximate place where the correct length is reached and directs close assessment to what comes before this. However, credit is given for relevant material appearing later.
Handwriting and Spelling	Poor handwriting, spelling errors or faulty punctuation are not specifically penalised but the overall impression mark may be adjusted if it is felt that communication is impeded.
Irrelevance	The examiners' first priority is to give credit for the candidates' efforts at communication, but candidates who introduce blatantly irrelevant material learned by heart or who deliberately misinterpret the question are penalised.
Background Reading Texts	In Question 5, the examiners are looking for evidence that candidates have read and appreciated a background reading text and are able to provide evidence of this in the form of illustrated description and discussion at an appropriately abstract level.
	Judgement of compositions set on a background reading text is based, as for other composition tasks, on control of language in the given context rather than on content or interpretation, though it is obviously necessary to downgrade candidates who attempt these topics without preparation.
Marking	The panel of examiners is divided into small teams, each with a very experienced examiner as Team Leader. The Chief Examiner guides and monitors the marking process. This begins with a meeting of the Chief Examiner and the Team Leaders. This is held immediately after the examination and begins the

Appendix II

process of establishing a common standard of assessment by the selection of sample scripts for all five questions in Paper 2. These are chosen to demonstrate the range of questions and different levels of competence and used for the preliminary co-ordination of marking of all examiners allocated scripts for that paper.

In the marking, each examiner is apportioned scripts chosen on a random basis from the whole entry, in batches of not more than fifty scripts, in order to ensure there is no concentration of good or weak scripts or of one large centre in the allocation of any one examiner. In addition to a rigorous process of co-ordination and checking during the marking itself, statistical moderation of examiner marks is carried out so that any subjectivity of marking is minimised.

The candidate's final score is out of 40.

Appendix II

SAMPLE PAPER: PAPER 2 COMPOSITION

Instructions to candidates:
Answer **two** questions.
All the questions carry equal marks.

1. Describe a person whom you regard as successful and define the qualities needed to achieve success. (About 350 words)

2. Nowadays people live longer than they did in the past. Discuss the advantages of living longer and the problems created by this situation. (About 350 words)

3. Write a story entitled *The Lost Diary*. (About 350 words)

4. There has been considerable noise caused by low-flying aircraft over the area where you live. Write to the airport authorities to complain and to explain the effect of the noise on you and your neighbours. Suggest what actions the authorities could take and what compensation they should offer. (About 350 words)

5. Based on your reading of **one** of these books, write on **one** of the following. (About 350 words)

(a) RUTH PRAWER JHABVALA: *Heat and Dust*
Discuss the reasons why Olivia left her husband and describe the effects this decision had on her family and friends.

(b) TIMOTHY MO: *Sour Sweet*
Describe how Chen becomes involved with the Wo Society and comment on how this affects him.

(c) WILLIAM GOLDING: *Lord of the Flies*
'Piggy is different from the other boys.' Use this statement to describe his character and the events which lead to his death.

Appendix II

Sample Candidate Scripts and Principal Examiner Comments

You are invited to look at the following sample compositions A and B, together with the marks awarded and the comments. You may then like to cover up the marks and comments on pages 35–38 and make your own assessments and then compare them with those awarded by the Chief Examiner.

Script A

Describe a person whom you regard as successful and define the qualities needed to achieve success.

In my oppinion Napoleon Bonaparte, who was historically a very important figure, was probably the most successful leader of the 19th century. His reign might not have lasted all that long compared to someone like Queen Victoria, but what he did achieve in his lifetime is quite admirable. It is amazing that an ordinary officer in the army could rise up out of the ranks and end up becoming Emperor of France and conquering almost all of Central Europe. Hid did not only use force to gain control over several contries but also his political know-how.

His military brilliance could be likened to that of one of history's other great conquerers Alexander the Great. His political genious which probably saved him from using unneccesary military force on a lot of occasions was remarkable. Time and time again he outwhitted his enemies by chosing the right allies at the right time so that the enemy had no choice but to agree to whatever he wanted.

Not only did he gain so much power over such a large area of Europe, but he also managed to solve the social, political and economic problems which France had been trying to deal with for several decades. The revolution was caused by these problems and it was supposed to solve them.

The revolution failed miserably and had created more problems than it was supposed to solve. This gave Napoleon the change to seize power and subsequently irradicate all of France's promlems. This made him extremely popular with the people of France and the followed him every inch of the way.

The reason why it was Napoleon who managed to pull France out of the rutt it was in, and not some other person is quite simple. As well as being a vary determined and ruthless man which he probably learned in the army, he had an extremely accurate sense of timing when it came to decision.

To be successful the most important qualities you must have are a good sense of timing, determination, sociable and you must have enough knowledge about whatever you are dealing with, preferebly more than your rivals.

The language used in this essay is assured and natural. There is a good range of appropriate vocabulary and idiomatic expression (*'political know-how'*; *'pull France out of the rut'*; *'extremely accurate sense of timing'*; *'created more problems than it was*

Appendix II

supposed to solve' etc.) marred to some extent by poor spelling. The sentence structure is good. There are many well-ordered complex sentences which read like those of a native speaker (*'outwitted his enemies ... by choosing ... so that ... no choice but to agree'; 'not only ... but also'* etc.).

The writer has been less successful in the realisation of the task. The question is in two parts – the second demands generalisations about the qualities needed to achieve success. Although the writer has recognised this, the second part of the question is not well developed; the task is attempted but the concentration is on the descriptive/narrative element.

It would be a more successful composition if both parts or aspects were dealt with equally – ideally with a progression/linking/development which demonstrates that the full task has been understood and realised.

Mark: 12

Appendix II

Script B

Nowadays people live longer than they did in the past. Discuss the advantages of living longer and the problems created by this situation.

> Thanks to the progress made by mediciine and the improvement of lifestyles, nowadays people have a much longer life expectation than their ancesters. Moreover the length of life is still progessing. Reaching the age of 120 will not be exeptional by the end of the next century.
>
> Already, people can enjoy a better life than their parents. They can choose to have children later, in order to make the most of their youth. When life was shorter, people did not have time to travel and develop their personality. Life was entirely devoted to working and building a family.
>
> Nowadays, at the age of retirement, people do not feel as tired as they used to. they are no longer considered as old. Indeed, recently retired people often get involved in voluntary work. For example they can make others benefit from their experience and skills by becoming teachers. More often, a hobby acquired during active lifetime is developped to a high degree of expertise. Therefore it is commonly accepted that retirement must be prepared several years in advance. The more active people are while working, the more likely they are to enjoy a fulfiling retirement.
>
> For that reason, people prepare more activiey for their future. This attitude has given use to a dramatic change in people's attitude towards life. leisure is taking an increasing importance. Having a successful career is still regarded as vital, but achieving personal balance has become a general expectation. In doing so, active people intend to prepare themselves for a period of retirement during which they will still be fit and capable of enjoying their former activities.
>
> This radical change is bound to generate a growing problem in western societies. the age of the population is rising. Therefore the number of pensioners per worker is growing. This trend faces modern societies with an increasing problem of funding. The issue is made even more acute by the fact that older people cost more interms of health expenditure. Each year, developed countries allow an increasing part of their national products to health.
>
> For fear of letting general dissatisfaction install, governments will have to address the problem, and it will probably imply drastic steps and changes.

The language used in this essay is generally competent and assured. There are some natural and appropriately used expressions (*'the more active people are while working, the more likely they are ...'; 'this attitude has given rise to ...'; 'this radical change is bound to generate'*), but also some lexical confusion, particularly with verbs (*'they can make others benefit'; 'this trend faces modern society with ...'; 'developed countries allows an increasing part'; 'it will probably imply drastic steps'* etc.).

Appendix II

The task is recognised and dealt with. The strengths of this essay are organisation; relevance to the topic chosen; appropriate vocabulary and expression; clarity of ideas and of the ways in which they have been ordered and set down. The errors are occasional rather than pervasive and, perhaps, arise more from the candidate's desire to set out thoughtful and extensive observations on the topic than to an inability to construct more mundane but very correct statements/observations which would be the mark of a less well-developed composition. The number of words misused does, however, bring the mark down.

Mark: 14

Appendix II

Script C
Write a story entitled **"The Lost Diary"**.

For years now, Helen has been confiding in her diary. For her, it meant more than just a book in which you are writing the event of your day. it was a friend, a very close friend who was listening to all her secrets thoughts without never disapointing her. Her first diary had been given to her by her mother for her birthday when she was seven years old. Now at seventeen, she had a collection of diaries. Some she had bought herself others were presents from family of friends. It was difficult for other to imagine being without one. Every night before going to bed she would take the time to relive her day and extract what was the more important. How did she feel when her mother gave birth to her sister! She was ten years old at the time. Losing the attention has been difficult. How did she overcome the death of her best friend from leucemia. The little dispute or quarrels with her schoolmaster, or teacher or parents. What she taught about music, her favourite actor or movie, her first kiss. Everything was in her diary.

Recently, she had meet a very nice guy with whom she was starting to feel more and more comfortable. She had met him in a party. He was the neighbor of one of her friend. Helen was quite shy and had problems sometimes to communicate with others. She knew that, but couldn't understnad why it was so difficult. When she was writing in her diary, it seems all so easy. As soon as she saw him, she felt inadequate with nothing to say. She had to force herself to participate in the conversation. With time, it became easier and they where now good friends. He knew about her diary and was encouraging her to confide more in him than in her book. But every night, Helen, meticulously, was writing about the progression of her feelings for Tim in her diary. One day, a tragedy happened. Let say a tragedy for Helen. She lost her bag and her diary was in it. It did not matter that she had lost her money and other belongings all it matters was that she had lost her diary. That one was very precious, it was about her feelings for Tim, it was about how she related to him and all the hopes she had for the future. She was devastated and looked everywhere to find it. It was somewhere to be found. She had the impression that her life had stopped and couldn't accept the lost. Everyone was very concerned about the reaction.

Finally, her freind Tim was a good help. She started to tell him more about herself and they both agreed that she was going through a kind of bereavement over a period of her life when she needed to put in writing all her feelings because she thought that nobody could understand. She will buy another one and she will continue to write in it but she did not feel as if it was the only thing that matter anymore. She will do her best to relate to others around her. She would seek everybodoy's help and write her diary for pleasure in future.

The language here does not reach the standard required at CPE level. In several places there are problems with verb tenses (*'losing the attention has been difficult'*; *'when she was writing in her diary, it seems all so easy'*, etc.). Expression is generally lim-

Appendix II

ited to a succession of simple sentences. Although there are few basic errors in syntax or grammar, the language is stilted and unnatural (*'the little dispute or quarrels'; 'had problems to communicate'; 'all it matters was that she had lost'; 'Tim was a good help'* etc.). The range of vocabulary is reasonable but there are careless slips (*'where', 'freind', 'the lost'*).

The task has been well attempted, resulting in a carefully constructed narrative, but it has been marked down because of the problems with language, especially the poor sequencing of tenses.

The length of the essay may also have a negative effect on the reader, in particular the slightly incoherent middle paragraph.

Mark: 10

Appendix II

Script D
Write a story entitled **"The Lost Diary"**.

> She sat herself down in her favourite chair with the pale blue ragged book she found in the attic. Outside the rain was pelting down, but she didn't take notice to eegre to read the diary she just found. When she opened it she noticed that a few pages was torn out and so there was no date on the first page.
>
> "... and the air was warm and still exept from the cool breeze, which came from the sea. The only thing I can hear is laughter in a distance, probably from one of the bungalows futher down the beach. As I sit herre admireing the scenary that lay before me with the ocean and the sky, which meet at a orange horizone. I think about times passed and time to be. Will I ever be able to get over him? Probably, but never forget. I can see someone walking down the shore, cannot yet tell if it's a man or a woman ... it's a man. I cannot see his face, but he's wearing a t-shirt and a pair of shorts, no shoes. As he walks along the shore, leaving footprints in the soft sand, flushed away by the silence of the waves, leaving no trace whatsoever. The beach looks as untuched as ever. I can see his face now, he looks troubled, something else aswell, but I cannot distinguish if it is angre or grief. I don't think he can see me, sitting here under a palm tree, but I can see him from here and quite clearly. Now, he sat down on the beach side, on a big rock. A rock that has been worne by the eternal tide, since the beginning of times, until it has become rounded and soft as velvet. Turning seaward he looks out over the big blue sea, without really seeing its splendour and indescribable beauty.
>
> A bird's shreek somewhere nearby and I can hear the rattle of leaves when it leaves its nest, then the night gets all quiet again. The man seems not to have heard the bird, he must be deep in thought.
>
> All of the sudden he rises and as if the thought, which had prayed upon his mind, had flew away like the bird, his face is no longer troubled. Instead he appears to be filled withy decorious exitment and for a short while his face looks ten years younger. He walks away, the same way he came from, leaving naked footprints in the sand. Agin the light waves flushes them away and leave the shore without a trace. Was i dreaming? Anyhow, the man or the illusion made me feel happier in one way, but on the same way more depressed and lonlier...'

This essay is marred by basic errors of many kinds – subject/verb agreement, verb forms, misuse of prepositions, spelling. In addition it is **not** a story about a lost diary – a diary is merely mentioned in the first paragraph as having been found, and is then quoted from at length. For this reason the answer is marked down for gross irrelevance. This is, perhaps, a remembered essay which has not been successfully adapted to this title.

The language and expression would put this into the 5–7 band, but the content brings

Appendix II

the mark down further. Rehearsed compositions are unfortunately sometimes a feature of the 'story' question – and are easy to identify by their lack of direction and appropriateness. In this example the language control and attempt at the task are both clearly inadequate for CPE.

Mark: 4

Appendix II

Script E

There has been considerable noise caused by low-flying aircraft over the area where you live. Write to the airport authorities to complain and to explain the effect of the noise on you and your neighbours. Suggest what actions the authorities could take and what compensation they should offer.

(date)   (Name and address)

Dear Sirs,
Recently I came to know that you plan to increase the number of aircraft activities in the next year. So far, this neighbourhood I live in has suffered considerably by the effect of low-flying aircraft noise. When I first moved to this house, without actually being told of the noise pollution by the former owner, the noise cost me several sleepless nights, and although that condition seems to have improved, often enough aircraft noise deeply disturbs me in my work as a musician who does recording at home.

Instead of actually increasing the aircraft activity, the appropriate action to take should be to decrease it considerably, just as much for environmental reasons, as planes are one of the greatest polluters of our air. Often enough, when I occasionally travel by plane myself, and so I am told by several other travellers as well, planes take off into the air with as much as half of the seats vacated.

Another fact is, or so I am informed, that a great number of planes are actually linking places which just as easily could be travelled by train, which does not take that much longer. I believe the main uses of inland flights ar businessmen with enough money and a paranoid fear of losing time.

Inland flights are not really necessary, and they inflict a considerable harm to the air we breathe in, the nights we sleep in, and, in my casse, our work as musicians.

I suppose the government substitutes these new plans, and as far as the existing aircrafts are concerned, the petrol they use, too. This money could be well spent into the currently bad state of the railway system.

I accept tht you cannot, and as a matter of interest, willnot cut the aircraft activities, but I urge you to reconsider and actual increase, as the harm done to my neighbourhood and all our environnment would be enormous.
Yours sincerely,

                         (signature)

This letter of complaint begins with close reference to the rubric but soon becomes confused. A lack of language control is shown here by poor choice of vocabulary and by very awkward expression ('*has suffered by the effect*'; '*often enough when I occa-*

Appendix II

<u>sionally</u> *travel'; 'which just as easily could be travelled'; 'money could be well spent into...'*). Many of the comments made, for example those about railways and pollution, are irrelevant in this context. The writer offers only a vague suggestion for future action and makes no reference to compensation, although these are specifically asked for by the question. The topic is, therefore, neither extended nor explored. Organisation and paragraphing are poor.

For this type of question it is essential for the response to be appropriate to the specified target reader; to have the expression and vocabulary to do so; to be well-ordered and to cover or include all the parts or aspects of the topic area as indicated in the question wording.

Mark: 6

Appendix II

Script F

'Piggy is different from the other boys'. Use this statement to describe his character and the events which lead to his death.

Among other characters described in "Lord of the Flies" a reader's attention is immediately attracted by Piggy. He is a fat, short-sighted boy of an unprepossessive appearance. He is not as agile as Jack or Ralph and he does not share the other boys' delight in exploring the island at the beginning of their sojourn there.

There are also several internal features of Piggy that make him stand out from the group. To start with, he applies logical thinking when assessing the situation on the island. From the very start Piggy manipulates Ralph who is devoid of the ability of reasoning when confronting all the events on the island. For example, unlike Piggy he doesn't realise the danger of converting the boys' into savages by the authoritarian leadership of Jack.

Secondly, Piggy seems to be composed enough to control the changing events and never displays extreme reactions to them. He is calm enought to cheer up ralph after Simon's death and persuade him to believing that Simon was "batty" and "asked for it". This proves that his intellect is stronger than his conscience.

Another quality that differentiates Piggy from his peers is his sense of fairness. It can be seen in his attempts to introduce a set of rules preventing the boys from becoming "a pack of savages". Piggy is fair and expects the same from others. At the beginning he hopes Ralph will not divulge his nick-name to anybody. Shortly before his death he believes that Jack will give him back his glasses only because that is what fair conduct requires.

Lastly, Piggy's personality can also be regarded as unique because it is a mixture of both child-like and adult qualities. There is nobody on the island who would seriously consider sending a letter to the adult world or building a sun-dial. These ideas have a touch of adulthood but at the same time reveal childish naivety.

Piggy's death seems to be a natural consequence of his being different, particularly from Jack. Jack does not conceal his hostility to Piggy. He makes fun of his obese appearance calling him "fatty", he mugs him of his glasses and, at the end, does nothing to stop one of the hunters from dropping a piece of rock onto Piggy. The stages leading to his death are then very strongly linked with Jack's gradual coming to power.

All in all, Piggy's life illustrates the tragic conflict of the human with the wild, the democratic with the totalitarian and the reasonable with the instinctive. If we take all the facets of it into account it is no longer surprising that the outcome of it should be so tragic.

Appendix II

The language used here is very competent. There are occasional slips ('*several internal features of Piggy*'; '*calm enough to cheer up Ralph*'; '*mugs him of his glasses*') which betray that the writer's first language is not English, but generally the control is that of a native speaker. The writer uses a wide and varied vocabulary appropriately ('*sojourn*', '*devoid of*', '*differentiates*', '*authoritarian leadership*', '*facets*') and the essay is well organised into paragraphs.

The writer shows a thorough knowledge of the text and gives appropriate illustration, with reference to events ('*Simon's death*', '*loss of Piggy's glasses*' etc.) and quotation ('*pack of savages*', '*batty*', '*asked for it*' etc.). The essay answers all aspects of the question by explaining how Piggy is different and by referring to both character and events without straying into irrelevant, generalised observation. The final paragraph contains perceptive and interpretative comment.

It is a good example of an essay which focuses on the question set; is well-organised; moves from description to narrative to interpretation. It shows the ability to select and to give both illustrative detail and an overview, and has the language control and range to give a coherent and controlled piece of writing.

Mark: 18

APPENDIX III

The task is to carry out each of the following steps, which comprise the data preparation and collection phase:

- Task identification
- Task analysis
- Procedure selection
- Using supplementary data
- Data collection
- Data transcription

The two passages which follow are selections from two different EFL reading tests.

Appendix III

PASSAGE 1

Read the following newspaper article and then answer questions 16–21 on the next page. Indicate your answers on the separate answer sheet.

With the trees, I planted my stake in New Zealand

JONATHON PORRITT TALKS TO DANNY DANZIGER

Jonathon Porritt is the author of 'Seeing Green – The Politics of Ecology'.

I HAD a most peculiar period of my life when I didn't have any summers. I went out to New Zealand every summer here, which is the New Zealand winter, and so I had nine winters on the trot, which was great, because I like winter.

My parents came up with this idea of buying a small plot of land which 'the kids', my brother, sister and I, could look after. Mother said, 'If you can take the time and trouble to plant it with trees then you can have it.' The idea was that we would always have a stake in New Zealand, which is a lovely idea as my father was actually brought up there. And they found a plot of land about 20 miles north of Auckland in a place called Rangitoupuni. It's rather poor land, really, but it's quite good for planting trees on.

I've always been very keen and enthusiastic about land. I'd spent a year in Australia working on sheep stations and helping out in different farming jobs, and so the idea of planting trees sounded like a very nice idea, and I was immediately keen. I think the rest of the family got enthusiastic as we went along. I started planting in 1968, and by the end of 1972 between the three of us we'd planted the whole 70 acres.

In New Zealand in 1968 it was one of those winters. It rained an awful lot, endlessly in fact, and in a way it's idiotic to think back on it as such an immensely happy time as it rained pretty well most days that we were planting, and I don't suppose I've ever been wetter or colder for such a prolonged period.

There was a moment of truth every morning: getting ready for the next planting session. Coming out of the Land Rover relatively warm and dry, with the rain coming down, and your anorak still clammy from the day before, boots still sodden, hands fumbling with slippery laces.

'The brain begins to take over and to allow for all sorts of strange thoughts, ideas and reflections about life.'

In that first year I had a guy to work with me who was an experienced tree planter, which was

157

Appendix III

very helpful as I'd never planted trees seriously before all this. You have a planting bag around your neck which you fill with as many trees as you possibly can, and when your bag is full it's a nightmare, and it's only as it gets lighter that life gets easier.

In a way, the most difficult bit of the entire operation was getting the lines straight. You work out what spacing you're going to plant the trees at, and then you line up a series of three poles across as long a trajectory as you can get, and those poles then determine your lines. Once you're in line, you just plant all the way down the line till you get to the end, turn around and come back again. I enjoy hard physical work, and it certainly made me fit.

After a certain point you can plant trees almost on automatic, you become used to a rhythm, and you use the minimum number of spade strokes that you need to get the hole in the ground. The rhythm is something that everybody tells you about and, of course, it's true of many agricultural jobs that you actually have to train the body into a series of quite standardised moves, and then it becomes immensely easy: so you develop an absolutely regular process of taking the tree out of the bag, digging a hole, putting it in the ground, stamping it in, and moving on. Mentally, it's very interesting. The brain begins to take over and to allow for all sorts of strange thoughts and ideas and reflections about life – a lot of my thinking about the natural world and our place in it, all of those things that have since dominated my life, first began to pop through my head in those days.

I've been back to New Zealand four times since then and watched the trees gradually grow, which has been very satisfying when you actually planted the things and you do then have a kind of stake in what happens and how they prosper.

I always dread reading in the newspapers stories of another high wind in New Zealand, or *Worst Drought Ever Hits New Zealand*. Such headlines make me feel extremely apprehensive. However, it worked out extremely well and those trees are now 20 years old, and in good fettle.

The only postscript I should add is that I took a term off from teaching, and I went back there in 1984, completely on my own for three months. And I wrote my first book there, *Seeing Green*. There's a little cabin on the tree farm which is fantastically basic, just a bed, a table and a chair. In the mornings I would do my writing; in the afternoons I would go off and prune the trees, and then do research in the evenings.

The connection between me and that area is still immensely strong. In many respects it's the place that I feel most closely identified with in terms of that link between people and the earth: it's a most powerful bond.

Appendix III

16 When the Porritts first considered buying a piece of land for their children to look after,

    A Jonathon's brother and sister needed encouraging.
    B Jonathon himself reacted positively.
    C the whole family was equally enthusiastic.
    D Jonathon's mother imposed unrealistic conditions.

17 When he started planting trees in 1968, Jonathon

    A was employed by an expert tree planter.
    B had experience of the work in Australia.
    C had only limited experience of tree planting.
    D had to learn from scratch how to do the job.

18 1968 was a happy time for Jonathon even though

    A the work was physically demanding.
    B he didn't like being separated from his family.
    C the weather was very unpleasant.
    D he didn't enjoy living alone.

19 When did Jonathon become efficient at planting trees?

    A when he put fewer trees in his planting bag
    B when he got used to the nature of the soil
    C when he knew how to set up a planting line
    D when he had become accustomed to the routine

20 Jonathon found planting trees to be

    A an opportunity to reflect on important issues.
    B an increasingly monotonous activity.
    C a way to escape from reality.
    D the best way of keeping himself fit.

21 What is Jonathon's present view of the place where he lived in New Zealand?

    A He would like to spend more time there.
    B He would like to write about it.
    C He intends to return there soon.
    D He has a strong commitment to it.

Appendix III

PASSAGE 2

Alone in the apartment, Polly continued typing for ten minutes, then stopped to reheat her coffee. For the first time she felt the disadvantages of having become Jeanne's room mate. She didn't like being blamed for not wanting to visit Ida and Cathy, who weren't really her friends, and would probably be happier if she didn't come so they could analyse her character the way they always did with people who weren't there. They talked in a kind of catty way, even in a bitchy way. Polly scowled, catching herself in a lapse of language. Jeanne, among others, had often pointed out how unfair it was that when women were compared to animals it was always unfavourably: *catty, cow, henpecked.* While for men the comparison was usually positive: *strong as a bull, cock of the walk.*

She turned on the tape recorder again and typed another page, then stopped, thinking of Jeanne again. She didn't like being called a workaholic, even affectionately. She didn't like being given permission not to see people she didn't want to see. It was, yes, as if she were a child, with a managing, overprotective mother.

Of course, when she really was a child, Polly never had an overprotective mother. Bea was only twenty when her daughter was born and she'd had trouble enough protecting herself. She looked out for Polly the way an older sister or a baby-sitter might have done, without anxiety, encouraging her to become independent as fast as possible. Later, when Polly's half-brothers came along, Bea had shown impulses towards overprotection, but her husband frustrated them; he didn't want his sons 'made into sissies'.

According to Elsa, Polly's former shrink, any close relationship between women could revive one's first and profoundest attachment, to one's mother. Physically, of course, Jeanne was nothing like Polly's mother. Bea Milner was much smaller, for one thing. But to a child, all grown women are large, and psychologically there were similarities: Jeanne, like Bea, was soft and feminine in manner and given to gently chiding Polly for her impulsiveness, hot temper and lack of tact. Elsa's view had been that Polly needed Jeanne to play this role because she hadn't had enough 'good mothering' as a child and that Jeanne needed to play it because she was a highly maternal woman without children.

But I'm not a child any more, Polly thought. I don't want mothering. Anyhow, I'm four years older than Jeanne; the whole idea is stupid. She poured her coffee and added less sugar than usual.

31 What did Polly resent?

    A Jeanne's attitude to her
    B Ida and Cathy's gossip
    C having to share a room
    D being talked about

32 Why did Polly scowl?

    A because she disliked Ida and Cathy
    B because she wouldn't be missed
    C because Jeanne had criticised the language she used
    D because she was irritated by the words she was using

33 What do we learn about Polly's childhood?

    A She had felt a lack of affection.
    B She had learned to look after herself.
    C She was often separated from her mother.
    D She resented the attention her half-brothers received.

34 Which of her step-father's opinions does Polly recall?

    A Boys need to be self-reliant
    B Mothers should treat all their children in the same way.
    C Girls are more emotional than boys.
    D Children should not be treated with affection.

35 In what respect did Jeanne resemble Polly's mother?

    A her impatience
    B her appearance
    C her manner of speaking
    D her level of intelligence

Appendix III

Guidance on how to approach this task

For task identification, we need only assure ourselves in this case that the tasks in question lend themselves to examination through verbal protocol analysis. We have already seen that comprehension tasks are suited to protocol studies.

The two sample tests are similar in style and both are multiple choice format. We cannot however assume that both tests measure the same ability on the basis of these fairly superficial comparisons.

Next, we consider a task analysis.

(a) Task analysis

The multiple choice format makes a task analysis a little easier because the range of possible answers for each question that are likely to be considered by test takers is specified. We need to examine the kinds of processes that lead the test taker to opt for either the key response or a distractor. Since both tests are assumed to measure reading, then the task analysis should identify the same kinds of units for analysis in both cases, and the same sorts of strategies that test takers might adopt. Recall that very broad categories are unlikely to wield a great deal of power in analysis.

(b) Procedure selection

We have recommended thus far that concurrent reports be used as far as possible. You may choose to use retrospective reports, provided certain precautions are taken. It is often useful to gather some preliminary protocols using both procedures in order to ascertain how well each suits the purpose.

(c) Using supplementary data

Next, the reader should consider whether supplementary data are to be gathered. In this case, supplementary data might include notes made by the test takers, marks in text and so forth, as well as a video tape of the proceeding.

(d) Data collection

We have emphasised the importance of adequate briefing, instructions and practice when verbal reports are to be used. In particular, care must be taken when prompting participants. Unless a mediated procedure is being used, prompting should be as unintrusive as possible. Providing participants with verbal or non-verbal feedback on performance, and correcting errors are obviously not wanted.

Appendix III

(e) Data transcription

Provided the equipment is all of a reasonable standard, you should be left with a batch of tapes for transcription. The most efficient way to achieve this is to employ the services of an audio-typist.

At the end of this exercise, you should have analysed the tasks, adopted an appropriate procedure for collecting the verbal reports, collected some verbal reports and transcribed the reports. We should emphasise that there is no single correct approach in carrying out this exercise. Different procedures will yield different data. Whichever procedure you do adopt, the same procedure should be used for **both** tasks in order to facilitate comparisons.

APPENDIX IV

Recall that your task is to do the following:

(i)   Develop a coding scheme for analysing the protocols.
(ii) Identify what the unit for analysis will be.
(iii) Segment the protocols.

First we present the instructions presented to the students. Next, we describe the task students were asked to complete with two sample protocols. Finally, we provide some guidance to help the reader carry out this task.

Instructions presented to students

Students approaching this task were asked to think aloud while reading and choosing an appropriate word or phrase to fill the gap. They were asked to work as a pair and to keep talking as they worked through the items.

The task presented to students

Sample FCE Cloze Test from Paper 3 (Use of English)

Fill in each of the numbered blanks in the following passage. Use only one word in each space.

Isambard Kingdom Brunel was a famous nineteenth-century engineer. He .... (1) born in 1806 in Portsmouth, a seaport in the South of England. In 1823, after studying .... (2) two years in Paris, he started .... (3) for his father, ... (4) was an engineer and inventor. He had been born near Rouen in France but in 1792 had left France for the USA and had later settled in England. Both father and son were responsible for the design .... (5) construction of the first tunnel under the River Thames. The digging of this tunnel was .... (6) in

Appendix IV

1825 and completed twenty years later. Today, it .... (7) part of the London Underground system.

Isambard Kingdom Brunel went .... (8) to design the *Great Britain* (1845), ... (9) was the first large ship to be built .... (10) iron instead of wood. It was powered .... (11) steam and made regular crossings of the Atlantic. Remarkably, this ship is .... (12) in existence. It .... (13) been restored and can be seen in Bristol, ... (14) it was originally built. .... (15) of Brunel's great engineering achievements was the construction of the Great Western Railway from London to Bristol. He designed all the stations, bridges, tunnels and viaducts along the line.

Brunel's ideas were ahead of his time and he had difficulty in convincing people that they were realistic, and, indeed, some of his projects were very ambitious, but he .... (16) determined to find .... (17) to the .... (18) difficult problems. Overwork ruined his health and he .... (19), at the early age of fifty-two, in 1859. The work of Brunel, and his father, has always been highly regarded and Brunel University, founded in 1966, is .... (20) after both of them.

The sample protocols
Pair A

Speaker 1:	Isambard Kingdom Brunel was a famous 19th century engineer. He was
Speaker 2:	Was! Was born
Speaker 1:	was born in Portsmouth, a seaport in the South of England. In 1823 after studying ... for? Two years in Paris. What do you think?
Speaker 2:	It could be after studying engineering. No.
Speaker 1:	Maybe, it's got to be for.
Speaker 2:	Got to be for
Speaker 1:	for two years in Paris, he started ... looking ... for his father:

165

Appendix IV

Speaker 2: Working.

Speaker 1: Yeah, OK, working for his father who ... was an engineer and inventor. He had been born near Rouen in France but in 1792 had left France for the USA and had later settled in England. Both father and son were responsible for the design ... and construction?

Speaker 2: Yeah

Speaker 1: of the first tunnel under the River Thames. The digging of this tunnel was ... completed ...

Speaker 2: No

Speaker 1: No, started

Speaker 2: Started

Speaker 1: started in 1825

Speaker 2: begun

Speaker 1: began! No, it can't be, it's was, was begun, it can't be ... that.

Speaker 2: It can be!

Speaker 1: You don't say, 'was begun'.

Speaker 2: was started.

Speaker 1: Yeah, OK! In 1825 and completed twenty years later. Today it ...

Speaker 2: remains

Speaker 1: Yeah, remains or is part of the London Underground system.

Appendix IV

Pair B

Speaker 1: Isambard Kingdom Brunel was a famous 19th century engineer. He was born in Portsmouth, a seaport in the South of England. In 1823 after studying for two years in Paris he started ... working for his father, who was an engineer and inventor. He had been born near Rouen in France but in 1792 had left France for the USA and had later settled in England. Both father and son were responsible for the design and construction of the first tunnel under the River Thames. The digging of this tunnel was ... completed ... in

Speaker 2: Ah, but then it says completed twenty years ...

Speaker 1: Oh. OK, the digging of this tunnel was ... started? Begun?

Speaker 2: Yeah.

Speaker 1: OK, started or begun in 1825 and completed twenty years later. Today it remains part of the London Underground system.

Pair C

Speaker 1: Isambard Kingdom Brunel was a famous 19th century engineer. He ...

Speaker 2: was

Speaker 1: was born in 1806 in Portsmouth, a seaport in the South of England. In 1823 after studying ... for ... two years in Paris?

Speaker 2: Yeah. Or it could be a subject or something he was studying, like engineering.

Speaker 1: But then you'd need 'for his' ...

Speaker 2: oh yeah, for his ...
Speaker 1: Yeah. Studying for two years in Paris, he started ...

Speaker 2: working?

Speaker 1: working for his father who was an engineer and inventor.

Appendix IV

	He had been born near Rouen in France but in 1972 ... in 1792! ... had left France for the USA and had later settled in England. Both father and son were responsible for the design and ...
Speaker 2:	and
Speaker 1:	construction of the first tunnel under the River Thames. The digging of this tunnel was ...
Speaker 2:	Started
Speaker 1:	started? Er ... is that right? Started?
Speaker 2:	Yeah.
Speaker 1:	Was, was begun maybe?
Speaker 2:	Um, I think started sounds better.
Speaker 1:	OK, in 1825 and completed twenty years later. Today it ...
Speaker 2:	Is
Speaker 1:	is part of the London Underground system.

Guidance on how to approach this task

The comments made here are general suggestions to help the reader decide how to carry out this task. It is important to bear in mind that there are no right or wrong answers here, and the reader should feel free to develop alternative ideas on coding and segmentation.

(a) Developing a coding scheme

The nature of the coding scheme will reflect the questions the study seeks to address. Thus, different coding schemes with different emphases might well arise.

For instance, the researcher may be interested in the ways in which different options for each item are considered and evaluated. In this case, we might look at each item in turn and consider the response to it, regardless of which

Appendix IV

of the two students actually generated the response.

If, on the other hand, the researcher is interested in social factors, such as the relative contributions made by the individual students, then one way to approach the development of a coding scheme might be to classify the different approaches to answering each item taken by each student. This would allow the researcher to compare what the two students say.

The nature of the coding categories themselves is of course task-dependent. In this case, it may be useful to start by considering the broad activities that each student engages in. For instance, a large chunk of each protocol excerpt may be classified as 'reading'. An apparently simple activity like reading is a good example because it actually comprises a range of distinct activities, all of which are geared towards the general goal of understanding. Thus, we can contrast a straightforward read-through with re-reading (or paraphrasing, although paraphrasing is likely to prove inappropriate for this particular task). Other activities may be broadly classified as 'selection of a response' and 'evaluation'. Questions might focus on whether an option is evaluated, and if it is, how it is evaluated. Which options are evaluated might also be a question to consider. What criteria, if any, are used to make a selection?

(b) Identifying the unit for analysis

The unit for analysis may also be influenced by the research questions to be addressed. A unit for analysis might be any excerpt of protocol generated by a single student, if a comparison between students is required. Alternatively, a unit for analysis may be the item itself, which would allow for comparisons between items. This sort of approach would be appropriate if the researcher was interested in item difficulty for instance. However, if each item stimulates more than a sentence of dialogue, a more fine-grained analysis may be appropriate, or even necessary to capture activities such as selection and evaluation of options.

(c) Segmentation

The process of segmentation is usually straightforward once the unit for analysis has been identified. If the focus is on verbalisations of each individual, segmentation may proceed by identifying who said what, and segmenting the protocol accordingly. Alternatively, if the unit for analysis is an item, then individual items should be delineated and sectioned off. In either case, it is frequently preferable to carry out a more fine-grained analysis, and so segments within the verbalisations of each speaker, or within each item, may be identified and marked.

Subject Index

A
activity descriptions, 42, 60, 66
ALTE, 35
applications for VPA, 2–3, 13–14, 117–20
assessment categories, 24–25
    listening, 25, 30–31, 35–36, 40
    reading, 24–31, 34–37, 39–40, 67–72, 76–77, 96, 120
    speaking, 25, 34–38, 40
    translation, 25, 29, 37–38, 49, 73–74, 95
    writing, 25, 28, 34–36, 52–62, 64, 66, 70, 78–79, 81–84, 97–99
automating VPA
    automatic analysis, 52, 78, 100–103
    automatic coding, 52, 78, 100–102

B
bias, 11, 19, 92–93
briefing, 41, 50

C
Certificate in Advanced English, 53, 60–65, 85–86, 110
Certificate of Proficiency in English, 28, 61, 85
cloze test, 24, 91, 116
coding
    categories, 12, 18–19, 38–39, 68–78, 118
    schemes, 11–12, 14, 16, 18–19, 38–39, 56, 68–78, 118
cognitive processes, 1–4, 7–13, 18–20, 26–30, 36–37, 46, 53–59, 69–77, 84, 89, 98–100
cognitive skills, 2–4, 13–15, 21, 23, 74, 117, 119–120
construct validation
    concurrent criterion relatedness, 22–24, 27, 34
    concurrent validity, 22–24
    construct validity, 2–3, 13–15, 21–30, 34–35, 53, 117, 120
    content relevance and content coverage, 22–23
    content validity, 22–23

    convergent validity, 22–23
    criterion relatedness, 22–24, 27
    criterion validity, 22–23
    discriminant validity, 22–23
    face validity, 24, 27
    predictive utility, 22, 24
    predictive validity, 22–24
content analysis, 33, 119

D

data analysis techniques
    analysis of variance, 20, 96
    chi-square, 20, 96–97
    code-code transition frequencies, 96–98, 101
    correlation, 20, 105
    discriminant analysis, 96
    errors analysis, 23, 95, 99–100
    multidimensional scaling, 98
    profiling, 2, 97–8
    t-tests, 96
debriefing, 43
discourse analysis, 1, 25
disruption of behaviour, 5–6, 9–11, 20–21, 37, 42

E

encoder reliability, 12–13, 19, 71, 92
    inter-coder reliability, 68, 93–94, 101, 104, 111
    intra-coder reliability, 93–94, 101
equipment, 41, 43
experts, 2–4, 12

F

feedback, 16–17, 42, 66

G

guessing, 26, 36–37, 100

I

individual differences, 2–3, 11–12, 29, 74
instructions, 4, 7, 9, 11, 20–21, 41–48, 50, 59, 65–66
introspection, 4
item analysis, 3, 32, 34

Subject index

M
marking
 criteria, 3, 15, 64
 process, 3, 15, 39, 53, 5–58, 60–62, 64–65, 69–70
mediated procedures, 5–9, 16, 20, 41
metacomments, 82, 84, 89, 107, 109
multiple choice, 24, 26, 30

N
novices, 2–4, 12, 74

O
oral interview, 24, 41

P
paired reports or individual reports, 49–50
pauses, 6, 13, 17, 26, 42, 50–52, 73, 84
practice, 16–17, 42–44, 46–48, 50
pretesting, 32–34, 100
probes and prompting, 5, 9–10, 41–42, 50

Q
quantitative methods, 34

S
schema theory, 98, 118
segmenting, 13, 19, 51–52, 69–78, 84–85, 89–91, 101–102
sessions
 before the sessions, 41–42
 during the sessions, 42–43
 after the sessions, 43
short term memory, 7–8, 37
sparse reports, 21, 41, 51
supplementary data, 12, 15, 17, 31, 40–41

T
time markers, 17, 51–52, 60
TOEFL, 26
transcribing, 13, 15, 17, 31, 49–51, 60–66
trialling, 32–34

U
UNIX, 101

V
verbal protocols
    concurrent reports, 2, 4–6, 10–11, 16, 40–50, 59, 65, 119
    mediated reports, 4–7, 9, 16, 41
    retrospective reports, 2, 4–6, 10–11, 16, 40–48, 50, 65, 119
    talk aloud, 1–2, 4–10, 16, 41–48, 59, 65
    think aloud, 1–2, 4–10, 16, 41–48, 59–60, 65–66, 69, 73–74, 92, 96, 103

W
written recall protocol, 27

Author Index

Anderson, Farrell and Sauers, 2, 121
Bachman, 22, 24
Bachman, Davidson and Milanovic, 119
Ballstaedt and Mandl, 9
Bereiter and Scardamalia, 58–59, 121,
Bhaskar and Simon, 102, 121
Buck, 30, 32, 121
Chi, Glaser and Rees, 12
Cohen, 119, 121
Cronbach and Meehl, 22
Cumming, 119, 121
Deville and Chalhoub-Deville, 27, 122
Diederich, French and Carlton, 60, 122
Ericsson, 37
Ericsson and Simon, 7–8, 10–11, 19–20, 42–43, 59, 69, 98, 102
Flower and Hayes, 54
Freedle and Kostin, 26, 30, 122
Freedman, 60, 122
Gerloff, 38, 73–75, 122
Gilhooly, 21
Gilhooly and Green, C., 85, 101
Green, A.J.K., 117
Green, A.J.K., and Gilhooly 1990a, 2–3, 74, 76
Grobe, 60, 122
Hayes-Roth and Hayes-Roth, 29, 123
Hölscher and Möhle, 29, 123
Laszlo, Meutsch and Viehoff, 2, 123
Lazaraton, 25, 123
Messick, 22, 117, 123
Milanovic and Saville, 53, 60–61, 119, 123
Milanovic, Saville and Shen, 39, 61, 123
Milanovic, 31
Mislevy, 120, 123
Nisbett and Wilson, 11

Author index

Norman, 99, 123
Norris, 3, 9, 123
Payne and Squibb, 100, 123
Reason, 123
Scardamalia and Bereiter, 54, 121, 124
Schoenfeld, 2
Schoenfeld and Herrmann, 2, 12
Schvaneveldt, Durso, Goldsmith, Breen, Cooke, Tucker and De Maio, 124
Shohamy and Inbar, 30, 124
Stewart and Grobe, 60, 124
Thorndyke and Stasz, 2
Upshur, 24, 124
University of Cambridge Local Examinations Syndicate, 124
Voss, Greene, Post and Penner, 2, 124
Wijgh, 119, 124
Wood, 58, 124,